Rhythm Book 101 Quarter Note Rhythm Patterns

I0201708

Taura Eruera

Rhythm Book 101 Quarter Note Rhythm Patterns

Published by Hookmedia Co Ltd

Hookmedia Co Ltd

© Copyright Taura Eruera 2006. All Rights Reserved.

Email: hookmediapublications@gmail.com

National Library of New Zealand

ISBN 0-9582254-0-0
Kindle ISBN 0-9582254-1-9

Rhythm Book Series

Rhythm Book 101	Quarter Note Rhythm Patterns.	The *Dobodobo* Rhythms
Rhythm Book 102	Eighth Note Rhythm Patterns.	The *Dabadaba* Rhythms
Rhythm Book 103	Sixteenth Note Rhythm Patterns.	The *Dibidibi* Rhythms
Rhythm Book 104	Triplet Eighth Note Rhythm Patterns.	The *Pataka Pataka* Rhythms
Rhythm Book 105	Triplet Eighth Note Rhythm Patterns.	The Syncopated *Pataka Pataka* Rhythms
Rhythm Book 106	Quarter Note Rhythm Patterns.	The *Dobobo* Rhythms
Rhythm Book 107	Eighth Note Rhythm Patterns.	The *Dababa* Rhythms
Rhythm Book 201	Quarter Note Rhythm Patterns.	The *Dobodobo Dobodobo* Rhythms
Rhythm Book 202	Eighth Note Rhythm Patterns.	The *Dabadaba Dabadaba* Rhythms
Rhythm Book 203	Sixteenth Note Rhythm Patterns.	The *Dibidibi Dibidibi* Rhythms

For my parents: Wiri Toka Eruera, who could make any melody work against three chords and Martha Eruera, who gave me my first guitar.

"On the bandstand or in the rehearsal room, I never heard any musician ask another:"Hey! Is that 3e+a 4triplet. Rest rest 3?" More often I heard someone calling, "Hey! Is that doowy doowy didaly uh uh bweee?" And the other replying,"Yeah! You got it! Wadu wadu wataka boh boh yiii!"

Made me wonder why we were being taught to *count* rhythm in the classroom."

Taura Eruera

Contents

Introduction

Welcome to Rhythm Book 101 Quarter Note Rhythm Patterns for All Musicians.

In the next ninety-nine minutes, or so, you could contrive to read every word--and *talk* every rhythm--in this book. In less than seventeen minutes you can learn a dobodobo vocabulary of sixteen, quarter note, rhythms from scratch. Then, in the remaining time, using this vocabulary, you can--to your possible surprise and absolute delight--talk seven hundred and fifty-eight bars of dobodobo rhythms.

This book is a *doing* book. It is not a thinking book. I do not attempt to explain an experience you have not yet had. I give you an experience first, then invite you to reflect on what you learned from that.

To that end, my introductory comments will be as brief as possible. As I write I am keeping in mind the question: what is the *least* you need to know to successfully complete this book?

The first point to note is that this whole book is based on only *one rhythm*: the quarter note rhythm. This entire book is about talking quarter note rhythms *derived* from this one rhythm.

In this book we refer to this seed rhythm as the dobodobo rhythm. This parent rhythm is displayed here.

do   bo   do   bo

In this bar you see five horizontal lines, called a stave, a G treble clef, a 4/4 time signature and four quarter notes or four crotchets. All these aspects are lumped under the heading of music notation.

Under the first and third quarter notes is the syllable do. Under the second and fourth quarter notes is the syllable bo. The do vowel and bo vowel are pronounced the same as the vowel in go. Any syllable displaying under a note is called a rhythmisation syllable.

These syllables form the word dobodobo. Dobodobo is the rhythmisation for a bar of four quarter notes.

In the seven hundred and fifty-eight bars that follow I ask you to take no notice of the stave, clef and time signature. I ask you to focus only on the rhythm notes and rhythmisation.

Rhythmisation is to rhythm what solmisation (solfa or solfeggio) is to melodic pitch. Just as do re mi uniquely describes the sound of the first three notes of a major scale so does dobodobo *uniquely* describe a bar of four quarter notes.

Rhythmisation is a system for verbalising rhythm. Rhythmisation is the language we use to talk the dobodobo vocabulary in this book.

The dobodobo vocabulary consists of several rhythms *derived* from this seed rhythm.

We concern ourselves with only sixteen of them in this book.

When we talk about dobodobo we are talking about a rhythm *level*. When we talk about the dobodobo's, we are talking about the dobodobo rhythm *vocabulary*. When we talk about a dobodobo rhythm we are talking about any rhythm that is a *member* of this vocabulary.

Talking the sixteen rhythms is simple. **The dobodobo vocabulary uses three vowels** pronounced as follows: e as in bed, u as in blue, o as in go.

As you can see, vowel pronunciation is simple. Pronouncing vowel *duration* or vowel length is not so simple for native English speakers because vowel length is not significant in English conversation.

For example, if you say the word movie, with a really long o sound or a short one, the meaning remains the same. The upshot is that learning to talk five different durations for five different vowels is a new experience, for most monolingual English speakers.

All vowels are all different lengths.

The **o** vowel is one click or one beat long.

The **u** vowel is two clicks or two beats long.

The **e** vowel is four clicks or four beats long.

The **ou** and **uo** diphthongs are three clicks or three beats long.

Please note that in this book, one metronome click measures one beat.

The consonants, **d**, **b** and **s** are pronounced as normal.

Attacks and Syllables

In any rhythmisation vocabulary, the rhythms are grouped by *attacks*. An attack signals where any rhythm duration starts. Durations may be sounded or not sounded. A sounded duration is indicated by a d or b consonant. An unsounded duration is indicated by an s consonant.

The attack status of a rhythm does not count every syllable in a word. Only sounded syllables are counted. This is why *sobodobo* is counted as a three attack rhythm, *sudobo* as a two attack rhythm, *sobou* as a one attack rhythm and *se* as a nil attack rhythm.

The rhythms in the dobodobo vocabulary are presented in groups of 4 attacks, 3 attacks, 2 attacks, 1 attack and 0 attack rhythms.

Dobodobo Vocabulary in Notation and Rhythmisation

Here is the dobodobo vocabulary presented in notation and rhythmisation, grouped by attacks.

The Dobodobo Vocabulary

Rhythmisation by Taura Eruera

do bo do bo

3 Attacks

do bo bu   do bu   bo

du   do bo   so bo do bo

2 Attacks

do bou   du   bu   duo   bo

4

so bo bu   so bu   bo   su   do bo

1 Attack

de   so bou   su   bu   suo   bo

0 Attacks

se

Syncopated Rhythms

do bu bo   do bou   duo bo sobu bo   so   bou

5

Dobodobo Vocabulary in Rhythmisation

Here is the sixteen word vocabulary presented in rhythmisation only.

4 attacks: dobodobo.

3 attacks: dobobu, dobubo, dudobo, sobodobo.

2 attacks: dobou, dubu, duobo, sobobu, sobubo, sudobo.

1 attack: de, sobou, subu, suobo.

0 attack: se.

Syncopated rhythms: dobubo, dobou, duobo, dobobu, dobou.

How Do You Learn The Rhythm Words?

Because of the vowel duration challenges mentioned earlier, it is important that you take time to *actually* learn to pronounce each word in the vocabulary. By that, I mean, it's important that your brain *actually* encodes and archives each word *accurately,* that your brain can retrieve each rhythm word on demand, that your speech system can *accurately* articulate each word and say each word, correctly, on demand.

To build this skill, I recommend you turn your metronome on to MM60 and say each word 8 times. If you are saying each dobodobo word for the very first time, focus on relaxing all your speech muscles: lips, tongue and jaw as you accurately articulate each consonant, each vowel duration, each syllable and each rhythm word as a whole.

Notice how it feels to say each dobodobo word once, twice, four and eight times. Saying each word once *is* saying a one bar phrase. Saying it twice *is* saying a two bar, call and response phrase. Saying it four times *is* saying two, two bar, call and response phrases.

Saying any rhythm word eight times is effectively saying four, two bar, call and response phrases, or two, four bar, call and response phrases.

Notice the difference between saying a word on an odd bar and an even bar, a strong bar and a weak bar.

If you want detailed step by step instructions to follow, refer to the Learn 16 Dobodobo Words in 8 Bar Sections in the appendices after page 104. You can also learn the dobodobo sounds with notation on page VI of the appendices. At MM60 this process will take you just over sixteen minutes.

Assuming you have learned the vocabulary, you are now ready to talk the big lot of dobodobo's, all seven hundred and fifty-eight of them.

This is not as scary as it might sound. You have already spoken each word a minimum of eight times. Over the next fifty-one minutes you will talk each word in the dobodobo vocabulary, several times, in several different contexts.

You will talk dobodobo 32 times across the 758 bars.

You will talk 3 attack rhythms one hundred and eighty five times: namely, dobobu 41 times, dobubo 62 times, dudobo 41 times and sobodobo, 41 times.

You will talk 2 attack rhythms three hundred and twenty one times: specifically, dobou 65 times, dubu 44 times, duobo 64 times, sobobu 38 times, sobubo 66 times and sudobo, 44 times.

You will talk 1 attack rhythms one hundred and eighty five times: specifically, de 21 times, be 20 times, sobou 62 times, subu 41 times and suobo, 41 times. Finally you will talk se 35 times.

You now know a lot. You now know how to pronounce each dobodobo word. You know how many times you are going to say each word. You know you will be talking seven hundred and fifty-eight bars of dobodobo. You know you will talking three hundred and sixty-three two bar, call and response, dobodobo phrases.

You know it will take you fifty-one minutes to read seven hundred and fifty-eight bars with no break between chapters or seventy minutes with breaks.

You know it's time for you to now launch yourself. Good luck.

Go talk yourself some dobodobo.

Chapter One: Talk 8 Attack Rhythm

In this chapter you talk only one rhythm: dobodobo, the parent rhythm for this vocabulary. Dobodobo occurs on both the first and second bar, that is, on both the strong and weak bar.

Dobodobo is the seed rhythm that the other fifteen rhythms derive from. This is the fundamental rhythm that you need to articulate clearly and cleanly. In the initial stages, you will do so carefully and deliberately, then---after many, many repetitions over time---automatically.

In this chapter you want to really feel each beat clearly. Feel each do beat clearly. Feel each bo beat clearly. Feel it in your imagination, your speech and your body.

Feel the strong beat clearly. Feel the weak beat clearly. Feel the downbeat clearly. Feel the upbeat clearly.

Feeling each do beat and each bo beat clearly is fundamental to feeling *every* rhythm in the dobodobo vocabulary. This is the skill required to be able to articulate, and feel, *diphthong rhythms* like duobo, and syncopations like dobubo.

Notice the principle of rhythm alternation operating here, at the level of the beat and the bar. As you talk dobodobo, notice what you notice about these beat (dobo) and bar (strong-weak) alternations.

This 8 attack rhythm has a (4 + 4) rhythm profile. The (4 + 4) profile means that the two bar phrase is a 4 attack rhythm in the strong bar and a 4 attack rhythm in the weak bar.

Notice what is different within you as you say this rhythm. How does the strong bar feel to you? How does the weak bar feel to you? Why is the dobodobo dobodobo rhythm called an 8 attack rhythm?

Chapter Two: Talk 7 Attack Rhythms

In this chapter you are talking 7 attack rhythms. That is, all the dobodobo rhythms in this chapter display a rhythm density of 7 attacks. Rhythm density is a term that broadly describes how rhythmically active a rhythm phrase is.

You are talking only the first five words of the dobodobo vocabulary--in different combinations—in this chapter. Clearly articulating the dobo alternation you learned in chapter one helps you with talking your first syncopated rhythm in this book: the dobubo rhythm.

In this chapter you are experiencing two bar, *call and response* phrases. The rhythm in the strong, odd numbered bar is the *calling rhythm* while the rhythm in the weak, even numbered bar, is the *responding rhythm*.

The rhythms in section B are called CV rhythms. The CV letters are initials, standing for constant variable rhythm which, in turn, is shorthand, for a *constant rhythm* calling a *variable rhythm*. That is to say, in section B, a constant rhythm in a strong bar is answered by a variable rhythm in the weak bar.

In section C, the reverse occurs with VC phrasing. That is, a variable rhythm in the strong bar is answered by a constant rhythm in the weak bar.

In this chapter you are also being introduced to the concept of *rhythm profile*. In section B, the rhythm profile of these 7 attack rhythm phrases is (4 + 3). This means that there is a 4 attack rhythm being answered by a 3 attack rhythm.

In section C, the rhythm profile is (3 + 4): that is, a 3 attack rhythm on the strong bar is being answered by a 4 attack rhythm on the weak bar.

After you have talked these rhythm profiles, reflect on how (4 + 3) phrases felt the same and different to you, from (3 + 4) phrases? What did you notice?

B

3

7 Attack Rhythm (4+3) CV

do bo do bo do bo bu

5

do bo do bo do bu bo

7

do bo do bo du do bo

9

do bo do bo so bo do bo

12

C — 7 Attack Rhythm (3+4) VC

11
do   bo   bu   do   bo   do   bo

13
do   bu   bo   do   bo   do   bo

15
du   do   bo   do   bo   do   bo

17
so   bo   do   bo   do   bo   do   bo

Chapter Three: Talk 6 Attack Rhythms

In this chapter you are talking 6 attack rhythms. That is, all the rhythms in this chapter display a rhythm density of 6 attacks.

For the first time, you will talk the 2 attack rhythms in this chapter: dobou, dubu, duobo, sobobu, sobubo, sudobo; in combination with the, 4 attack, dobodobo rhythm.

Combining 2 attack rhythms with a 4 attack rhythm will offer you *rhythm balance* insights that (3 + 3) rhythms do not.

In chapter two you met the three attack, dobubo, syncopated rhythm. In this one you meet the two attack, sobubo, syncopated rhythm.

For the first time in this talking section, you are meeting the two important, two attack, diphthong rhythms: dobou and duobo.

These rhythms are two attack derivations of three attack, rhythms: specifically, dobou from dobobu, and duobo from dudobo (see appendices pages XVII-XIX for a detailed discussion of *derived rhythms*).

Repeatedly saying these rhythm pairs---dobobu, dobou and dudobo, duobo---will guide you to the correct pronunciation for the dobou and duobo diphthongs.

You will also talk more 3 attack phrases, as both CV and VC phrases. You will get lots of practise talking 3 attack dobodobo rhythms. Again, you will reflect on how 3 attack CV phrases feel the same, or different, to you, as 3 attack VC phrases.

At the end of this chapter, take a moment to reflect on how, in your experience, (4 + 2) rhythms are similar or different to (2 + 4) rhythms. What do you notice?

How do the (3 + 3) phrases compare and contrast with the (2 + 4) and (4 + 2) phrases. What do you notice?

D

6 Attack 2 Bar (4+2) Rhythms CV

do   bo   do   bo   do   bou

21

do   bo   do   bo   du   bu

23

do   bo   do   bo   duo   bo

25

do   bo   do   bo   so   bo   bu

27

do   bo   do   bo   so   bu   bo

29

do bo do bo su do bo

E

6 Attack 2 Bar (3+3) Rhythm VC

31

do bo bu do bo bu

33

do bu bo do bo bu

35

du do bo do bo bu

37

so　bo　do　bo　　do　bo　bu

39

do　bo　bu　　do　bu　　bo

41

do　bu　　bo　do　bu　　bo

43

du　　do　bo　do　bu　　bo

45

so　bo　do　bo　　do　bu　　bo

18

47

do   bo   bu   du   do   bo

49

do   bu   bo   du   do   bo

51

du   do   bo   du   do   bo

53

so   bo   do   bo   du   do   bo

55

do   bo   bu   so   bo   do   bo

57

do bu bo so bo do bo

59

du do bo so bo do bo

61

so bo do bo so bo do bo

F   6 Attack 2 Bar (3+3) Rhythms CV

63

do bo bu do bo bu

65

do bo bu do bu bo

67

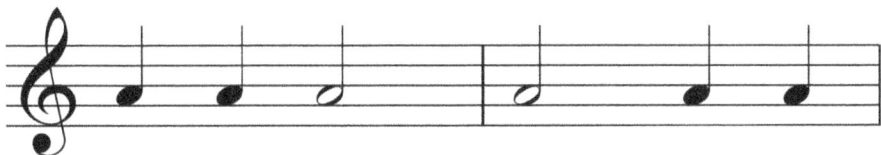

do　　bo　　bu　　　　du　　　do　　bo

69

do　　bo　　bu　　　　so　　bo　　do　　bo

71

do　　bu　　　bo　　　do　　bo　　bu

73

do　　bu　　　bo　　　do　　bu　　　bo

75

do　　bu　　　bo　　　du　　　do　　bo

77

do   bu   bo   so   bo   do   bo

79

du   do   bo   do   bo   bu

81

du   do   bo   do   bu   bo

83

du   do   bo   du   do   bo

85

du   do   bo   so   bo   do   bo

87

so bo do bo   do bo bu

89

so bo do bo   do bu   bo

91

so bo do bo   du   do bo

93

so bo do bo   so bo do bo

95

G   6 Attack 2 Bar (2+4) Rhythms VC

do bou   do bo do bo

97

du   bu   do bo do bo

99

duo   bo   do bo do bo

101

so bo bu   do bo do bo

103

so bu   bo   do bo do bo

105

su   do bo do bo do bo

Chapter Four: Talk 5 Attack Rhythms

In this chapter you will talk dobodobo rhythms with a rhythm density of 5 attacks.

For the first time, in this book, you will talk the 1 attack rhythms: de, sobou, subu and suobo; in combination with the 4 attack, dobodobo rhythm.

The two diphthong rhythms in this group are 1 attack derivations of 2 attack rhythms: specifically, sobou from dobou, and suobo from duobo. (see appendices pages XVII-XIX for details about derived rhythms).

Saying these rhythm pairs repeatedly---dobou, sobou and duobo, suobo---will guide you to the correct pronunciation for the sobou and suobo diphthong rhythms.

Rhythms like sobou, subu and suobo illustrate an important rhythm guideline: *rests are as important as sounded notes.* This ability to articulate rests, is one of the unique features of rhythmisation generally, and of dobodobo, specifically.

This feature protects the beginner student from the common beginners trap: ignoring rests altogether and focusing only on sounded notes.

In section H you are talking (4 + 1) CV phrases. How does the balance of the phrase feel to you when a 4 attack, strong bar, rhythm is answered by a 1 attack, weak bar rhythm?

Conversely, how does a (1 + 4) phrase in section K feel to you? What are the differences and similarities between a (1 + 4) and (4 + 1) phrase? How do the differences and similarities feel to you?

Similarly, in your experience, how do (3 + 2) VC rhythms in section I compare and contrast with (2 + 3) VC rhythms in section J?

In your view, how do (3 + 2) and (2 + 3) rhythms compare, and contrast, with (1 + 4) and (4 + 1) rhythms?

do   bo   do   bo   be

do   bo   do   bo   so   bou

do   bo   do   bo   su   bu

do   bo   do   bo   suo   bo

5 Attack (3+2) Rhythms VC

115

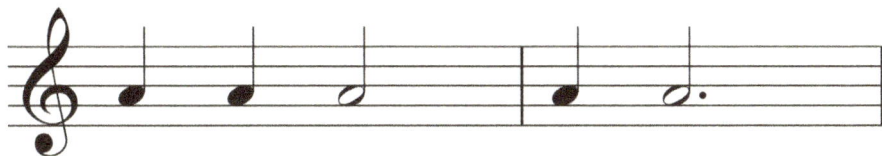

do   bo   bu   do   bou

117

do   bu   bo   do   bou

119

du   do   bo   do   bou

121

so   bo   do   bo   do   bou

123

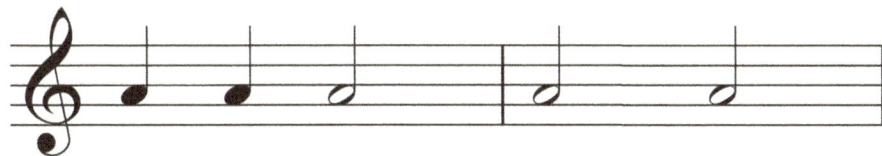

do   bo   bu   du   bu

125

do   bu   bo   du   bu

127

du   do bo   du   bu

129

so bo do bo   du   bu

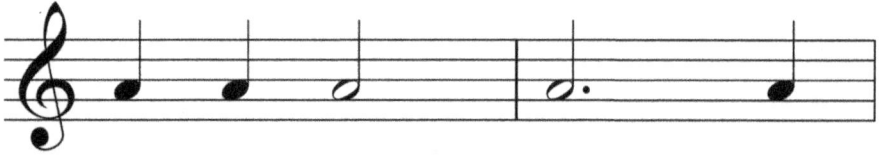

131

do bo bu   duo   bo

133

do bu   bo   duo   bo

135

du   do   bo   duo   bo

137

so   bo   do   bo   duo   bo

139

do   bo   bu   so   bo   bu

141

do   bu   bo   so   bo   bu

143

du   do   bo   so   bo   bu

145

so   bo   do   bo   so   bo   bu

147

do   bo   bu   so   bu   bo

149

do   bu   bo   so   bu   bo

151

du   do   bo   so   bu   bo

153

so   bo   do   bo   so   bu   bo

155

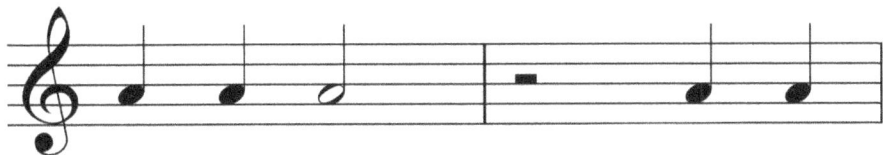

do bo bu su do bo

157

do bu bo su do bo

159

du do bo su do bo

161

so bo do bo su do bo

31

5 Attack (2 + 3) Rhythms CV

163

do   bou   do   bo   bu

165

do   bou   do   bu   bo

167

do   bou   du   do   bo

169

do   bou   so   bo   do   bo

171

du   bu   do   bo   bu

173

du   bu   do   bu   bo

175

du   bu   du   do   bo

177

du   bu   so   bo   do   bo

179

duo   bo   do   bo   bu

181

duo   bo   do   bu   bo

183

duo   bo   du   do   bo

185

duo   bo   so   bo   do   bo

187

so   bo   bu   do   bo   bu

189

so   bo   bu   do   bu   bo

191

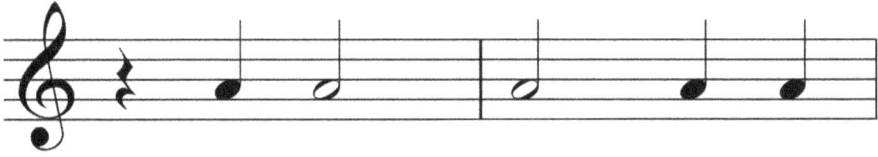

so   bo   bu   du   do   bo

193

so   bo   bu   so   bo   do   bo

195

so   bu   bo   do   bo   bu

197

so   bu   bo   do   bu   bo

199

so   bu   bo   du   do   bo

201

so bu bo so bo do bo

203

su do bo do bo bu

205

su do bo do bu bo

207

su do bo du do bo

209

su do bo so bo do bo

K

211

de   do   bo   do   bo

213

so   bou   do   bo   do   bo

215

su   bu   do   bo   do   bo

217

suo   bo   do   bo   do   bo

Chapter Five: Talk 4 Attack Rhythms

In this chapter you will talk only the dobodobo rhythms that have a rhythm density of 4 attacks.

For the first time, you talk the 0 attack rhythm, se, in this chapter: specifically, in the (4 + 0) and (0 +4) phrases. Again, take particular care in holding the e vowel for the full, 4 clicks duration. Nothing less than the full value will work.

With the introduction of se in this chapter, you have now talked all the rhythms in the dobodobo vocabulary. Congratulations. You will meet no more new rhythms in the remainder of this book: just new combinations.

In this chapter you have one hundred, 4 attack, dobodobo phrases, at your disposal. That is, you have ninety-nine dobodobo *rhythm variations* and substitutions available for any 4 attack dobodobo rhythm. Through the following profiles, you have one hundred ways to say a 4 attack dobodobo rhythm.

You have a (4 + 0) and a (0 + 4) phrase.

You have a selection of (3 + 1) CV and (1 + 3) VC phrases.

You have a selection of (2 + 2) VC and (2 + 2) CV phrases

Before you start talking these rhythms, think about what you expect the difference, between (4 + 0) and (0 + 4) phrases, to feel like to you. Similarly, what differences would you expect to experience with (3 + 1) CV and (1 + 3) VC dobodobo phrases? Again, what similarities and differences would you expect to experience with (2 + 2) VC and (2 + 2) CV dobodobo phrases?

At the end of this chapter, reflect on how your expectations lined up (or not) with your actual experience. This before-and-after process is not about finding any objectively right answer. It's about helping you think about rhythm and helping you describe *how* you think about rhythm.

A parting reminder: with the 1 attack and 2 attack rhythms, give great importance to articulating and saying the rest syllables--*in full*.

do bo do bo se

do bo bu be

do bu bo be

du do bo be

227

so   bo   do   bo   be

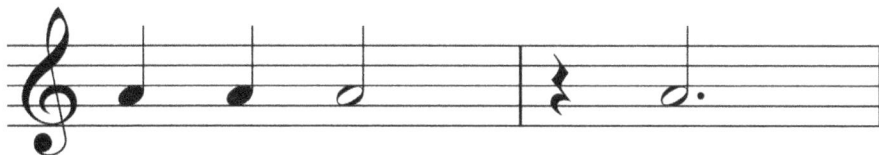

229

do   bo   bu   so   bou

231

do   bu   bo   so   bou

233

du   do   bo   so   bou

235

so   bo   do   bo   so   bou

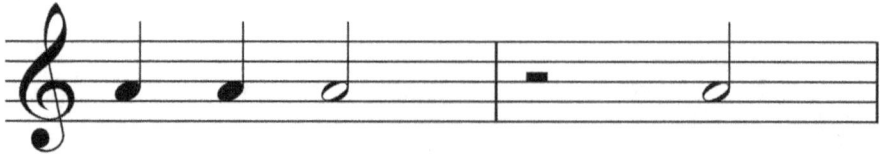

237

do   bo   bu   su   bu

239

do   bu   bo   su   bu

241

du   do   bo   su   bu

243

so   bo   do   bo   su   bu

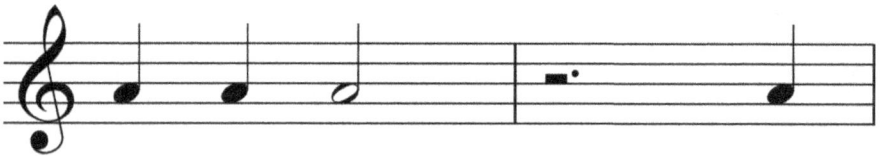

245

do   bo   bu   suo   bo

247

do   bu   bo   suo   bo

249

du   do   bo   suo   bo

251

so   bo   do   bo   suo   bo

N   4 Attacks 2 Bar (2+2) Rhythms VC

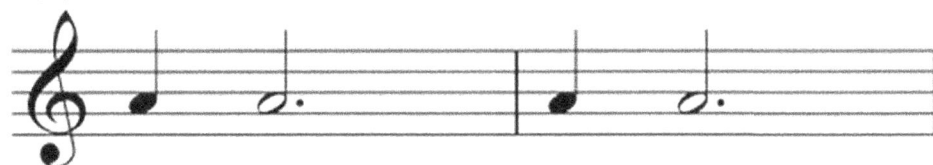

253

do   bou   do   bou

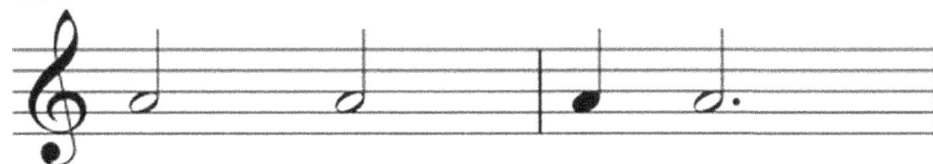

255

du   bu   do   bou

duo   bo   do   bou

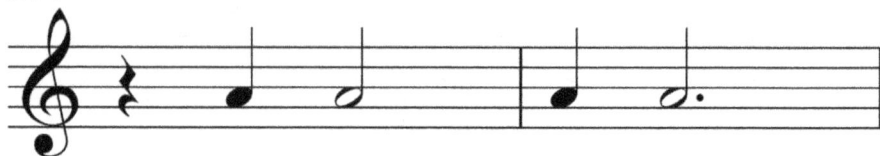

so   bo   bu   do   bou

so   bu   bo   do   bou

su   do   bo   do   bou

do   bou   du   bu

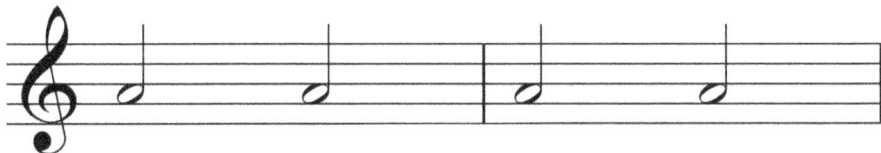

267

du   bu   du   bu

269

duo   bo   du   bu

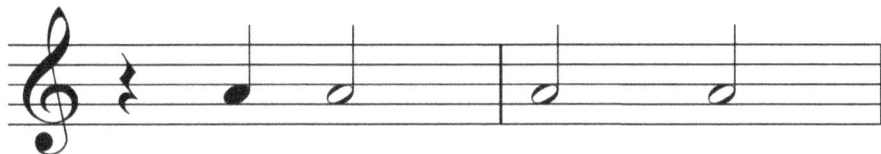

271

so   bo   bu   du   bu

273

so   bu   bo   du   bu

275

su   do   bo   du   bu

277

do   bou   duo   bo

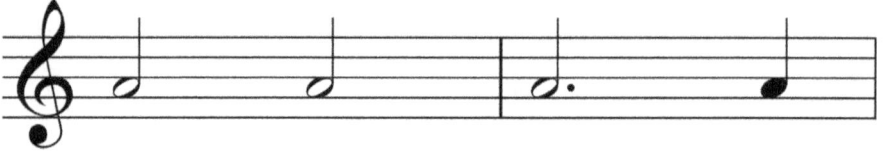

279

du   bu   duo   bo

281

duo   bo   duo   bo

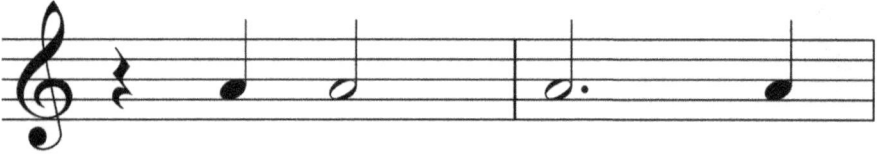

283

so   bo   bu   duo   bo

285

so   bu   bo   duo   bo

su   do   bo   duo   bo

do   bou   so   bo   bu

du   bu   so   bo   bu

duo   bo   so   bo   bu

so   bo   bu   so   bo   bu

297

so bu bo so bo bu

299

su do bo so bo bu

301

do bou so bu bo

303

du bu so bu bo

305

duo bo so bu bo

307

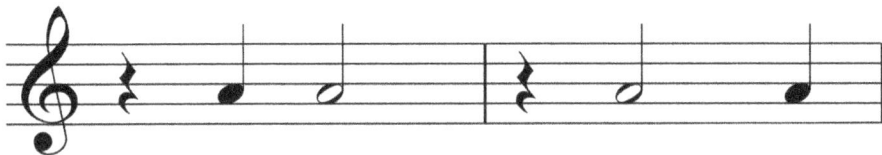

so   bo   bu   so   bu   bo

309

so   bu   bo   so   bu   bo

311

su   do   bo   so   bu   bo

313

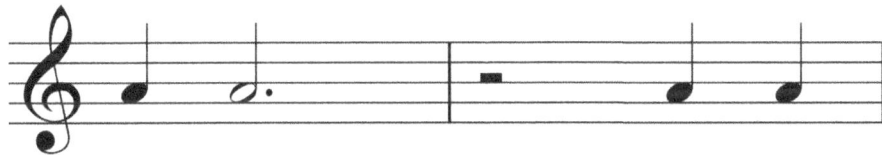

do   bou   su   do   bo

315

du   bu   su   do   bo

317

duo   bo   su   do   bo

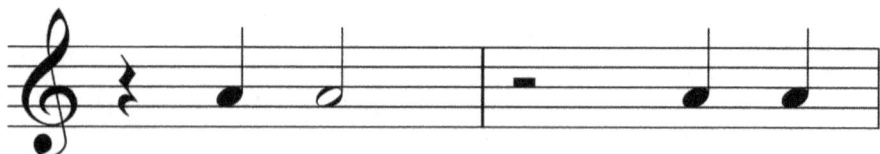

319

so   bo   bu   su   do   bo

321

so   bu   bo   su   do   bo

323

su   do   bo   su   do   bo

325

O

4 Attacks 2 Bar (2+2) Rhythms CV

do   bou   do   bou

327

do   bou   du   bu

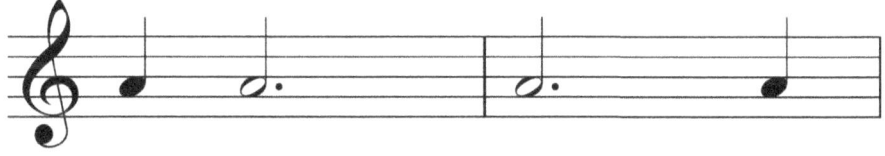

329

do   bou   duo   bo

331

do   bou   so   bo   bu

333

do bou so bu bo

335

do bou su do bo

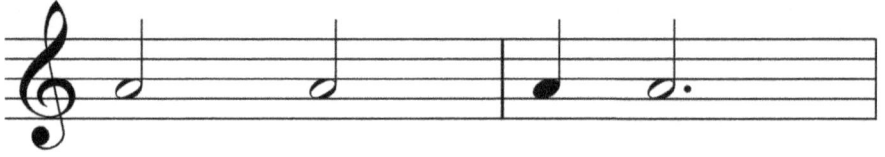

337

du bu do bou

339

du bu du bu

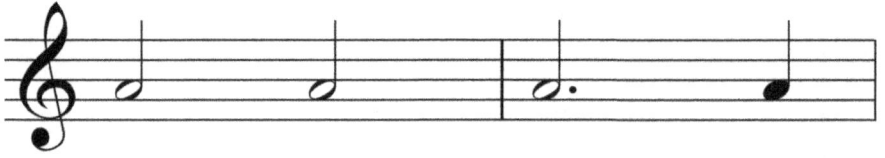

341

du bu duo bo

343

du   bu   so   bo   bu

345

du   bu   so   bu   bo

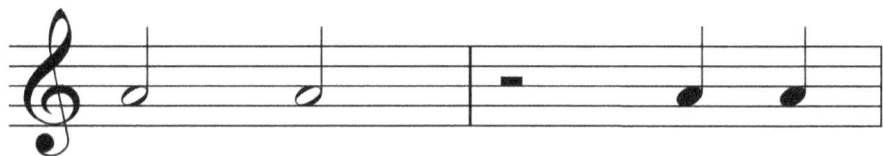

347

du   bu   su   do   bo

349

duo   bo   do   bou

351

duo   bo   du   bu

duo   bo   duo   bo

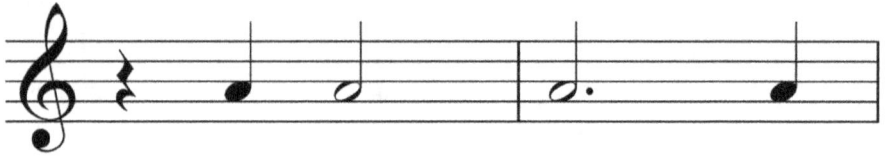

so   bo   bu   duo   bo

so   bu   bo   duo   bo

su   do   bo   so   bu   bo

do   bou   so   bu   bo

363

du   bu   so   bu   bo

365

duo   bo   so   bu   bo

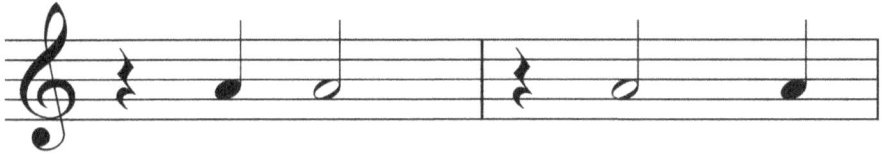

367

so   bo   bu   so   bu   bo

369

so   bu   bo   so   bu   bo

371

so   bu   bo   su   do   bo

373

su   do   bo   do   bou

375

su   do   bo   du   bu

377

su   do   bo   duo   bo

379

su   do   bo   so   bo   bu

381

su   do   bo   so   bu   bo

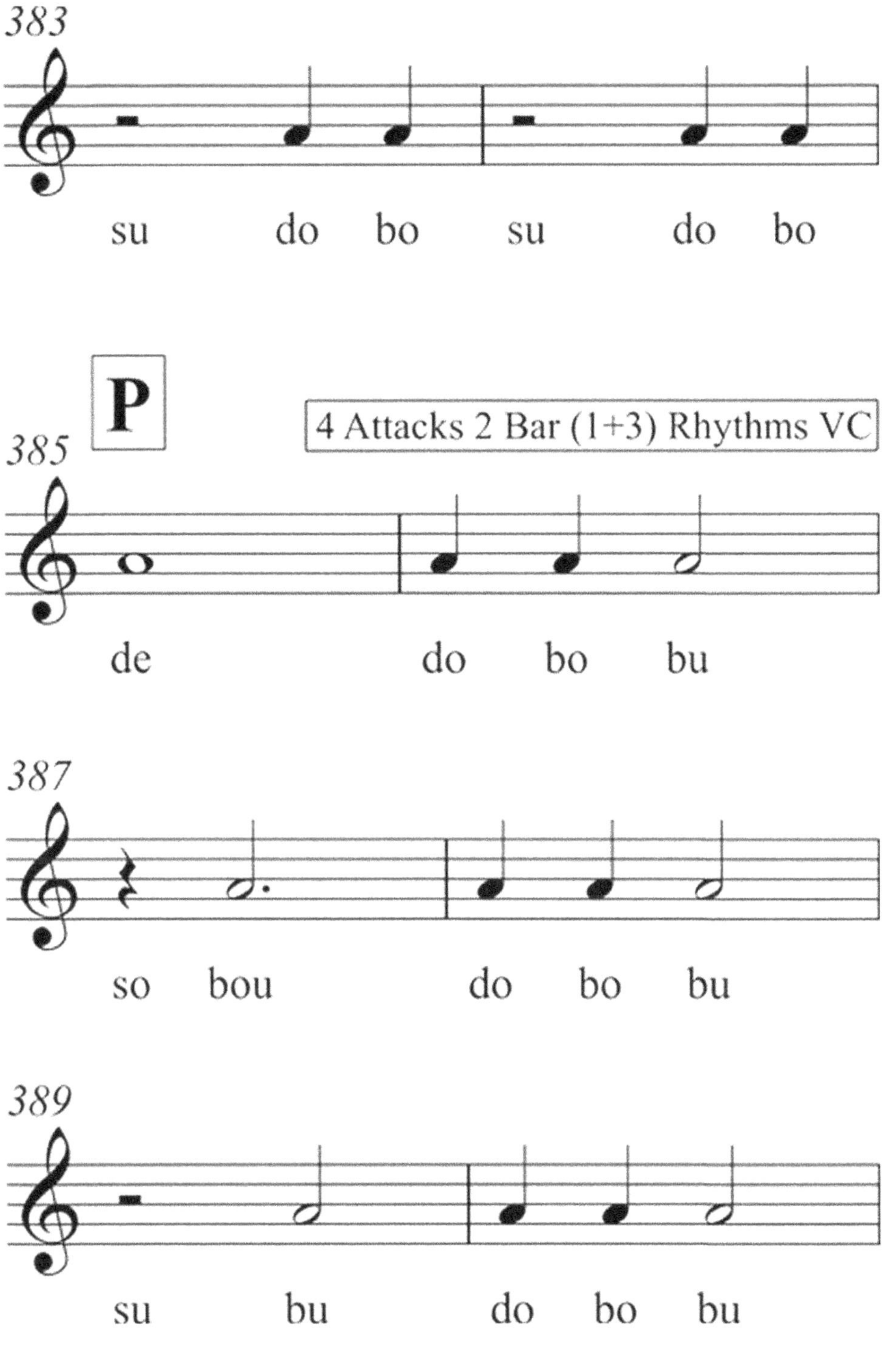

383

su   do   bo   su   do   bo

P

4 Attacks 2 Bar (1+3) Rhythms VC

385

de   do   bo   bu

387

so   bou   do   bo   bu

389

su   bu   do   bo   bu

391

suo   bo   do   bo   bu

393

de   do   bu   bo

395

so   bou   do   bu   bo

397

su   bu   do   bu   bo

399

suo   bo   do   bu   bo

401

de   du   do   bo

403

so   bou   du   do   bo

405

su   bu   du   do   bo

407

suo   bo   du   do   bo

409

de   so   bo   do   bo

411

so   bou   so   bo   do   bo

413

su   bu   so   bo   do   bo

415

suo   bo   so   bo   do   bo

417 **Q**   4 Attacks 2 Bar (0+4) Rhythms

se   do   bo   do   bo

Chapter Six: Talk 3 Attack Rhythms

In this chapter you will talk two bar, dobodobo phrases, with a rhythm density of 3 attacks.

With 3 attack rhythms, only three notes are being attacked across eight beats (and eight possible attacks). This means that five beats are not being attacked, and that these non-attacked spaces are being taken up with, either, long vowels, diphthongs or rests.

When you talk 3 attack rhythms you are, either, talking attacked long vowels or diphthongs--for their *full* duration—or, talking rested long vowels or diphthongs--for their *full* duration.

Generally speaking, the fewer the attacks employed, the more important the rests are. You must give primacy to accurately articulating the rests, the long vowels and diphthongs to make these rhythms work. Your pronunciation work in previous chapters will help you achieve this skill.

In this chapter you will talk (3 + 0) and (0 + 3) dobodobo phrases. You will also talk (2 + 1) CV and (1 + 2) VC quarter note phrases. You will have 58 different ways to express a 3 attack, dobodobo rhythm, and fifty-seven *rhythm substitutions* for, and variations on, any 3 attack, dobodobo rhythm. That's worth remembering any time you have a 3 attack melody to improvise on, or compose variations for.

Before you start talking these rhythms, think about what you expect the difference between a (3 + 0) and a (0 + 3) dobodobo rhythm to feel like. Similarly, what differences would you expect to experience with (2 + 1) CV and (1 + 2) VC quarter note phrases?

After you have talked this chapter, reflect on the same questions and see how your expectations lined up, or not, with your actual experience. Take note of your insights and how they help you think about rhythm in and out of tempo.

The advice to nail the rhythms in this chapter is always worth repeating. Pay close attention to articulating rests and tied vowels *in full*.

419 **R** 3 Attacks 1 Bar Rhythms

do bo bu do bu bo

421

du do bo so bo do bo

423 **S** 3 Attacks 2 Bar (3+0) Rhythms VC

do bo bu se

425

do bu bo se

427

du do bo se

429

so　　bo　　do　　bo　　　se

T　　　　　3 Attacks 2 Bar (2+1) Rhythms CV

431

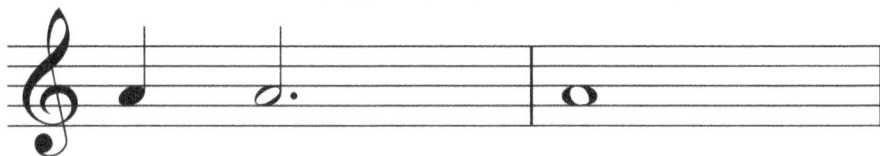

do　　bou　　　　　be

433

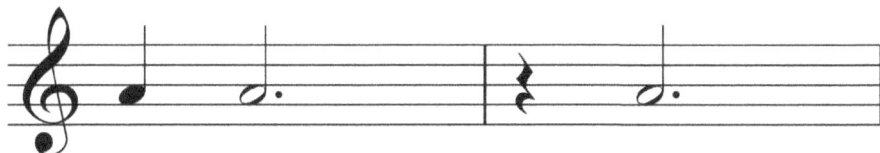

do　　bou　　　　so　　bou

435

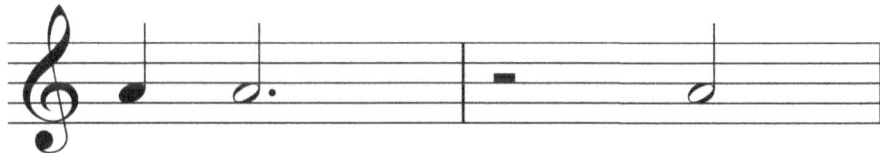

do　　bou　　　su　　　　bu

437

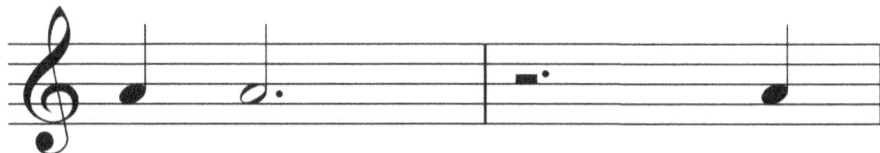

do　　bou　　　suo　　　bo

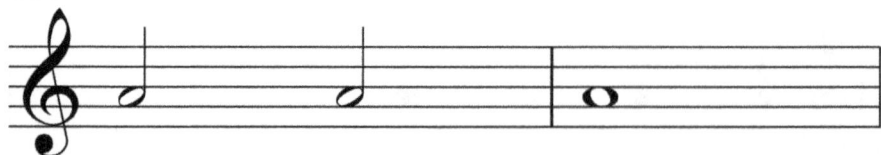

439

du   bu   be

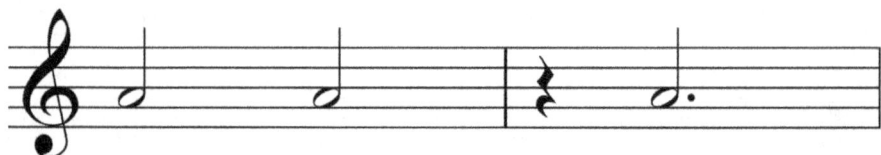

441

du   bu   so   bou

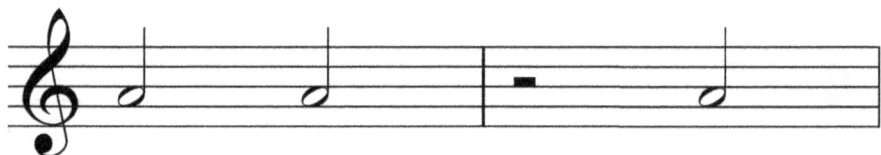

443

du   bu   su   bu

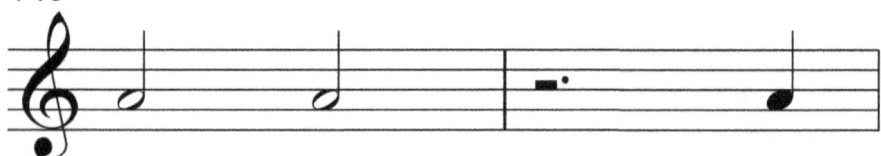

445

du   bu   suo   bo

447

duo   bo   be

duo   bo   so   bou

duo   bo   su   bu

duo   bo   suo   bo

so   bo   bu   be

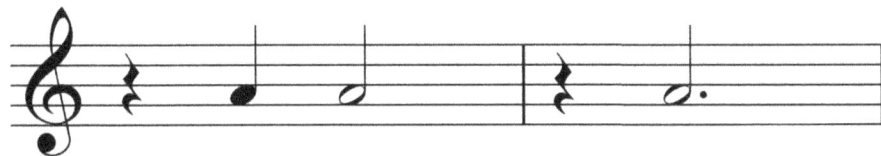

so   bo   bu   so   bou

459

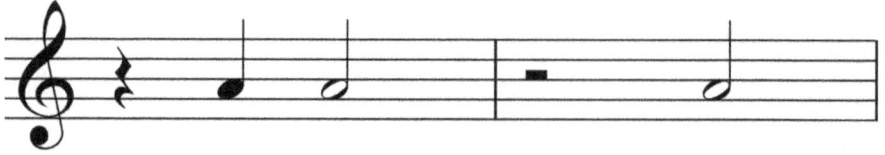

so   bo   bu   su   bu

461

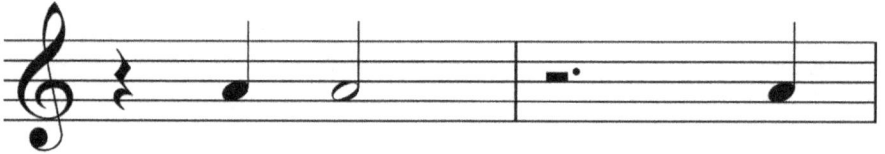

so   bo   bu   suo   bo

463

465 so   bu   bo   be

so   bu   bo   so   bou

467

so   bu   bo   su   bu

469

so bu bo suo bo

471

su do bo be

473

su do bo so bou

475

su do bo su bu

477

su do bo suo bo

U |3 Attacks 2 Bar (1 + 2) Rhythms CV|

de   do   bou

481

de   du   bu

483

de   duo   bo

485

de   so   bo   bu

487

de   so   bu   bo

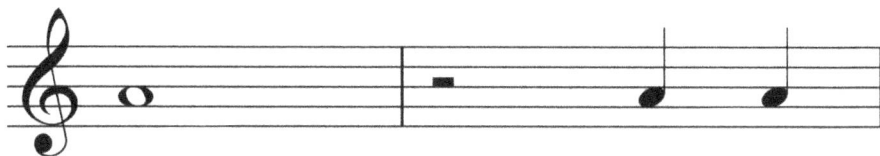

de   su   do   bo

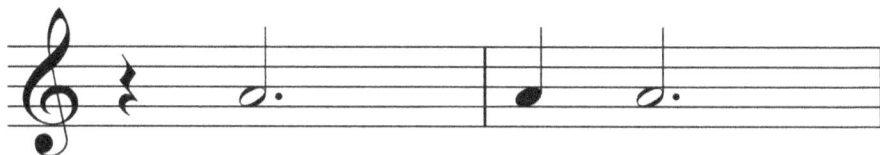

so   bou   do   bou

so   bou   du   bu

so   bou   duo   bo

so   bou   so   bo   bu

so   bou   so   bu   bo

so   bou   su   do   bo

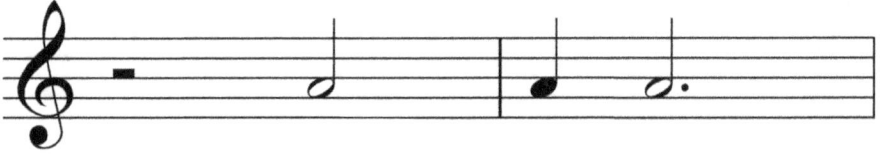

su   bu   do   bou

su   bu   du   bu

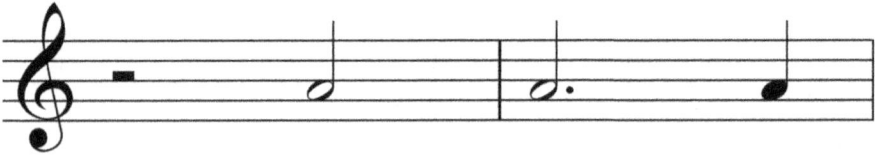

su   bu   duo   bo

509

su   bu   so   bo   bu

511

su   bu   so   bu   bo

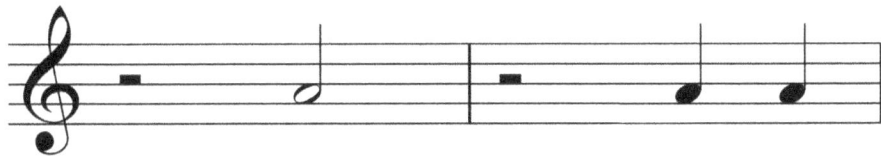

513

su   bu   su   do   bo

515

suo   bo   do   bou

517

suo   bo   du   bu

519

suo   bo   duo   bo

521

suo   bo   so   bo   bu

523

suo   bo   so   bu   bo

525

suo   bo   su   do   bo

V

527

3 Attacks 2 Bar (0 + 3) Rhythms CV

se   do   bo   bu

529

se   do   bu   bo

531

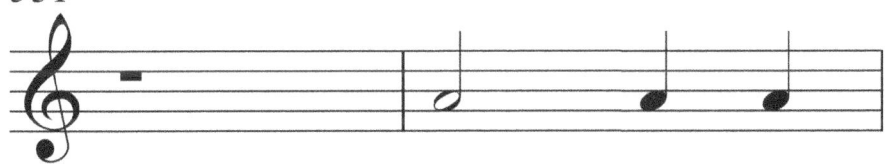

se   du   do   bo

533

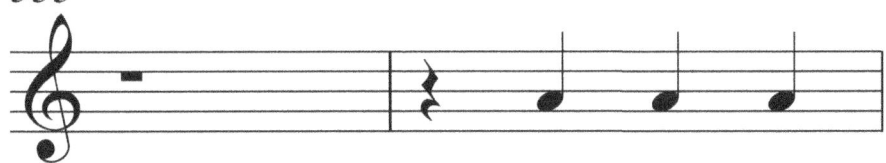

se   so   bo   do   bo

Chapter Seven: Talk 2 Attack Rhythms

In this chapter you talk dobodobo rhythms with a rhythm density of 2 attacks.

This means only two notes per two bar phrase are being attacked while six beats are not being attacked. These non-attacked beats are being occupied by long vowels, diphthongs or rests.

With 2 attack rhythms you are, either, talking attacked vowels or diphthongs--for their *full* duration — or, talking rested vowels or diphthongs--for their *full* duration.

With 2 attack rhythms, articulating rests and tied vowels or diphthongs accurately, are critically important to making these dobodobo rhythms work. Fortunately, you met these rhythms in chapter two. Your five chapters of experience — in articulating 2 attack rhythms — will help you.

You met 1 attack rhythms in chapter four. You have two chapters of experience — in articulating 1 attack rhythms--to bring to this chapter.

In this chapter, you will talk (1 + 0) and (0 + 1) dobodobo phrases. You will also talk (1 + 1) VC and (1 + 1) CV quarter note phrases. You will have 94 different ways to express a 2 attack rhythm and ninety-three rhythm substitutes for, and variations on, any 2 attack dobodobo rhythm.

As you anticipate talking these rhythms, think about what you expect the difference between a (2 + 0) and a (0 + 2) dobodobo phrase to feel like. Similarly, what differences would you expect to notice with (2 + 1) CV and (1 + 2) VC dobodobo phrases?

After you have talked this chapter, reflect on these same questions. Do your expectations line up, or not, with your actual experience? How do your observations help you think about rhythm, in and out of tempo?

The advice to nail the rests in this chapter is always worth repeating. Pay attention to accurately articulating rests, vowels and diphthongs — *in full.*

535 **W**

do   bou   du   bu

537

duo   bo   so   bo   bu

539

so   bu   bo   su   do   bo

541 **X**

2 Attack2 Bar (2+0) Rhythms VC

do   bou   se

543

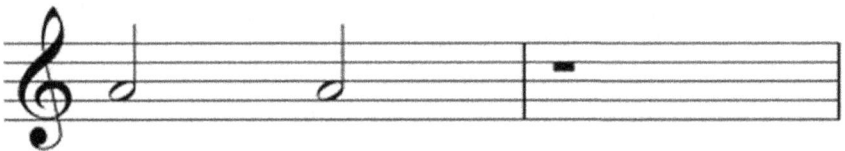

du   bu   se

545

duo   bo   se

547

so   bo   bu   se

549

so   bu   bo   se

551

su   do   bo   se

Y

2 Attacks 2 Bar (1+1) Rhythms VC

553

de   be

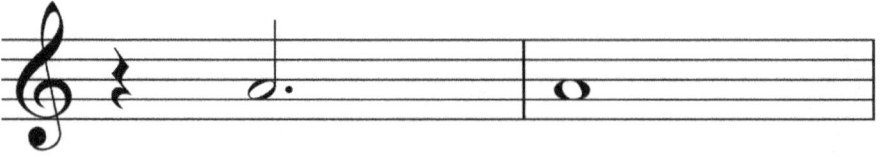

555

so bou be

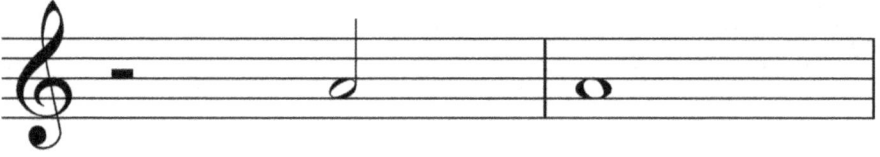

557

su bu be

559

suo bo be

561

de so bou

563

so bou so bu

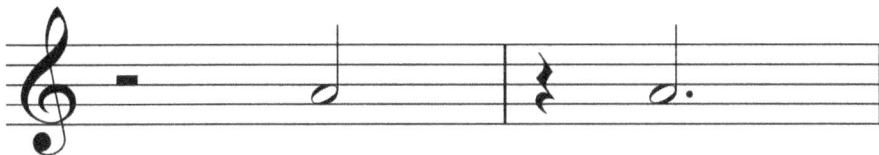

565

su   bu   so   bou

567

suo   bo   so   bou

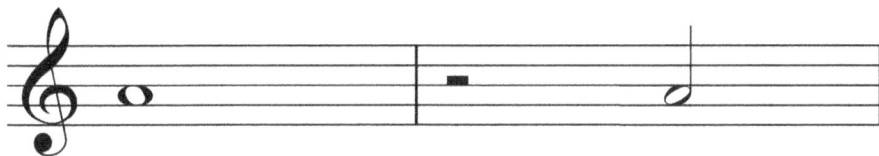

569

de   su   bu

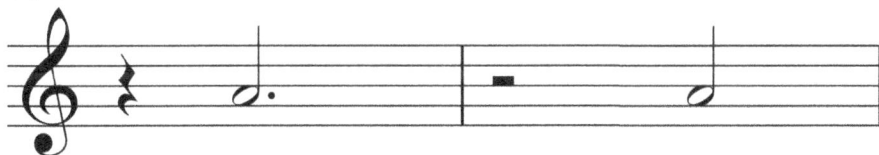

571

so   bou   su   bu

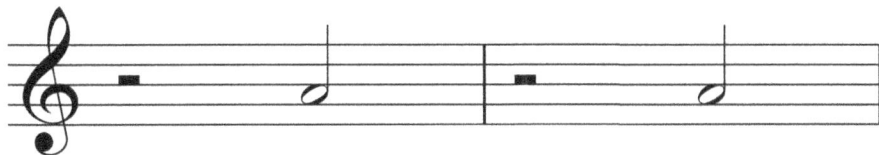

573

su   bu   su   bu

575

suo   bo   su   bu

577

de   suo   bo

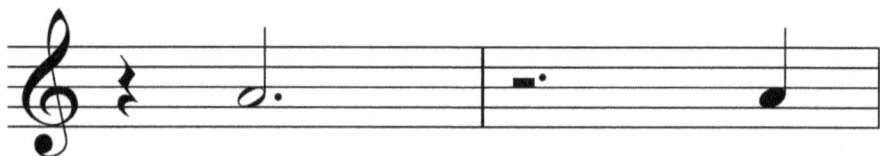

579

so   bou   suo   bo

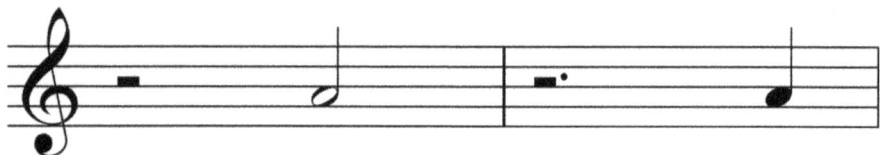

581

su   bu   suo   bo

583

suo   bo   suo   bo

585 **Z**

de   be

587

de   so   bou

589

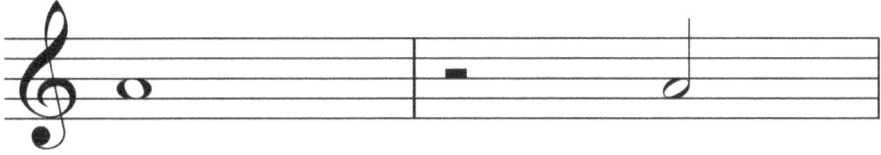

de   su   bu

591

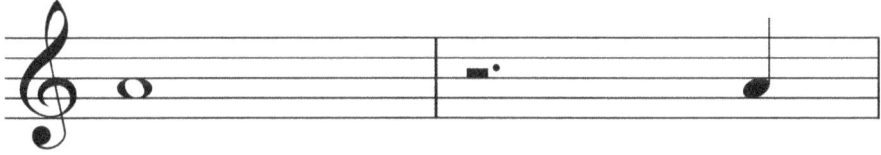

de   suo   bo

593

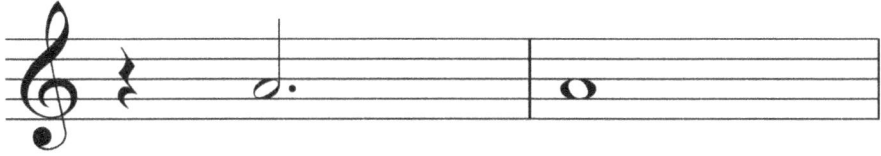

so   bou   be

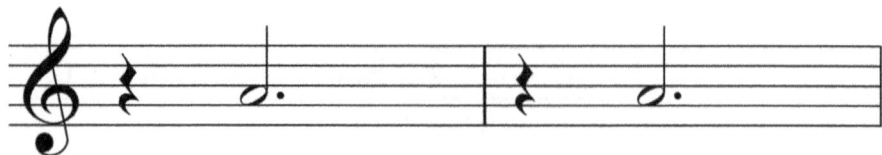

595

so   bou   so   bou

597

so   bou   su   bu

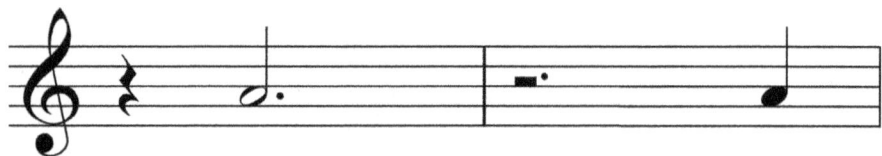

599

so   bou   suo   bo

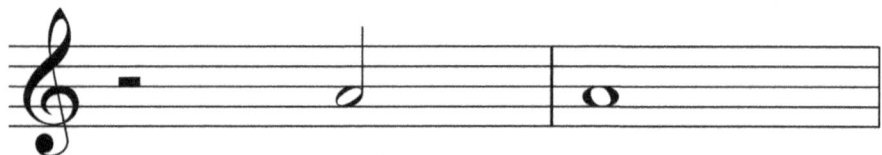

601

su   bu   be

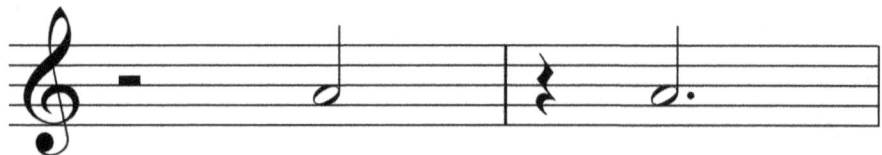

603

su   bu   so   bou

605

su   bu   su   bu

607

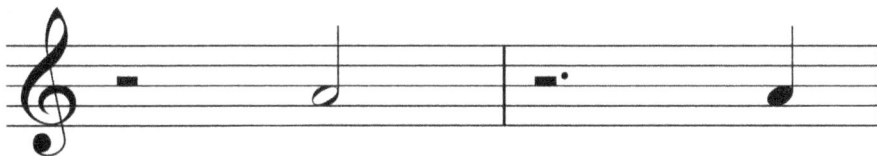

su   bu   suo   bo

609

suo   bo   be

611

suo   bo   so   bou

613

suo   bo   su   bu

615

suo   bo   suo   bo

AA   2 Attack2 Bar (0+2) Rhythms CV

617

se   do bou

619

se   du   bu

621

se   duo   bo

623

se   so   bo   bu

625

se   so   bu   bo

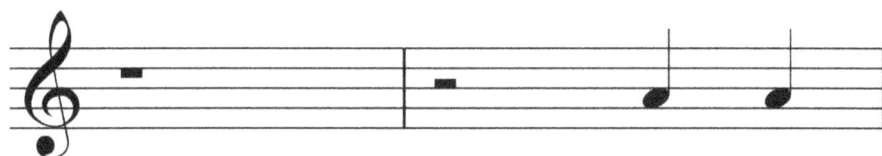

627

se   su   do   bo

Chapter Eight: Talk 1 Attack Rhythms

In this chapter you talk two bar, dobodobo rhythms, with a rhythm density of 1 attack.

When you talk one attack, dobodobo rhythms, across two bars, you notice that seven beats are not being attacked--and that these non-attacked beats are being occupied with, either, a long vowel, diphthongs or rests.

With 1 attack rhythms you are talking a one attack, long vowel, or diphthong--for the *full* duration — or, articulating a rest vowel or a diphthong--for the *full* duration.

With 1 attack, dobodobo phrases, articulating rests and tied vowels or diphthongs are *critically* important to making these rhythms work.

Learning to feel comfortable with the space around 1 attack rhythms is one of the benefits students report to me, after working with these rhythms. They also say they are much more aware of rhythm placement when they have only one note to work with.

In this chapter you will talk (1 + 0) and (0 + 1) dobodobo phrases. You will have eight different ways to express a 1 attack rhythm and seven rhythm substitutes for, and variations on, any 1 attack, dobodobo rhythm.

This might be useful to know when you need to come up with a variety of 1 attack rhythm hits for a song arrangement. This might be good to know, too, when you need to improvise a rhythm comment, in real time on your instrument, with only 1 attack.

As you prepare to talk these rhythms, think about what you expect the difference between (1 + 0) and (0 + 1) dobodobo phrases to feel like.

When you finish talking this chapter, reflect on these same questions. Did your expectations line up with your actual experience or not? Did this experience offer you fresh insights about rhythm, in and out of tempo?

Pay close attention to articulating rests and tied vowels--*in full*. Make the rests so accurate that the single attack just pops right out at you!

BB — 1 Attack 1 Bar Rhythms

629

de so bou

631

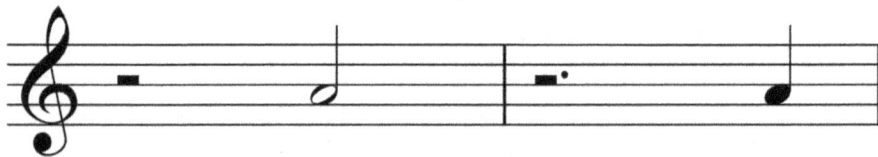

su bu suo bo

CC — 1 Attack 2 Bar (1+0) Rhythms VC

633

de se

635

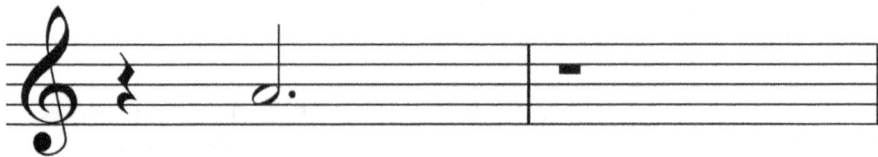

so bou se

637

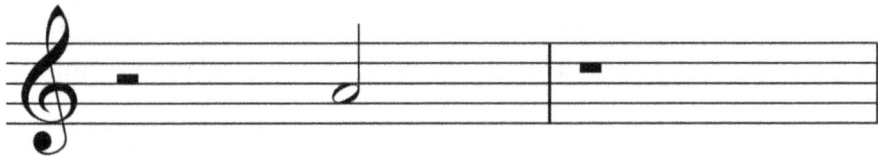

su bu se

639

suo   bo   se

DD   1 Attack 2 Bar (0+1) Rhythms CV

641

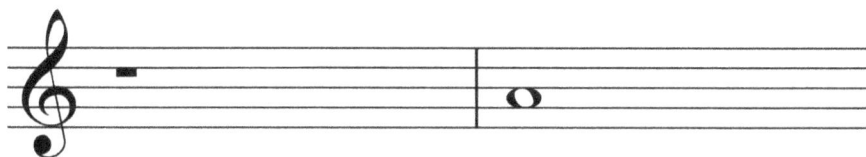

se   be

643

se   so   bou

645

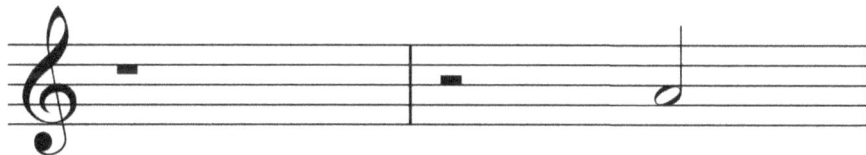

se   su   bu

647

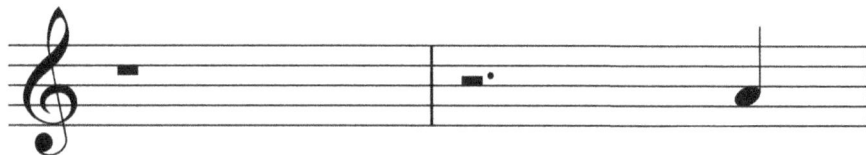

se   suo   bo

Chapter Nine: Talk Syncopated Rhythms

In this chapter you will talk only syncopated dobodobo rhythms. The five syncopated rhythms, native to the dobodobo vocabulary, isolated for you here, are bars 3, 6, 8, 10 and 13.

You have met all these syncopated rhythms in previous chapters: dobubo, dobou, duobo, sobubo and sobou. While these rhythms are not new to you; how they combine with each other, in two bar, syncopated, dobodobo phrases, will be.

Although they are not explicitly organised by rhythmic density in this chapter, it is clear that there is one, 3 attack syncopated rhythm; three, 2 attack syncopated rhythms; and one, 1 attack syncopated rhythm.

In section EE there are five variable syncopated rhythms occurring in the strong bar while a su rest occupies the weak bar.

In section FF the variable syncopated rhythm occurs on the strong bar and the constant syncopated rhythm answers in the weak bar.

In section GG the constant syncopated rhythm occurs on the strong bar and the variable syncopated rhythm answers in the weak bar.

You have these unmarked, dobodobo, rhythm profiles available to you in this chapter: (3 + 0), (3 + 1), (3 + 2), (2 + 2), (2 + 2), (2 + 3), (1 + 3) and (0 + 3). You have fifty-five, syncopated, dobodobo phrases available to you in this chapter.

Defining syncopation is not as useful as talking syncopation at this stage. Rather than come up with some definition it's more useful for you to be able to say: "Here are the syncopated rhythms in the dobodobo vocabulary; dobubo, dobou, duobo, sobubo and sobou."

You can say, think and feel these syncopated rhythms in tempo. You can't do that with a definition.

do   bu   bo   se

651

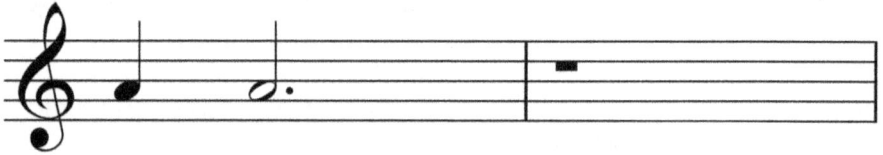

653   do   bou   se

duo   bo   se

655

so   bu   bo   se

657

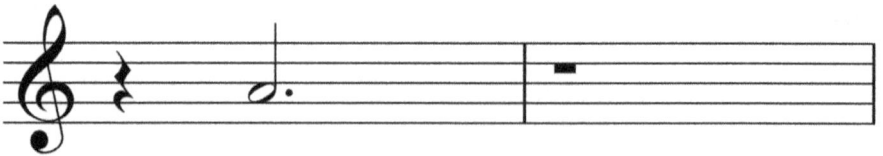

so   bou   se

FF

659

Repeat Rhythms on weak bars

do   bu   bo   do   bu   bo

661

do   bou   do   bu   bo

663

duo   bo   do   bu   bo

665

so   bu   bo   do   bu   bo

667

so   bou   do   bu   bo

669

do   bu   bo   do   bou

671

do   bou   do   bou

673

duo   bo   do   bou

675

so   bu   bo   do   bou

677

so   bou   do   bou

679

do   bu   bo   duo   bo

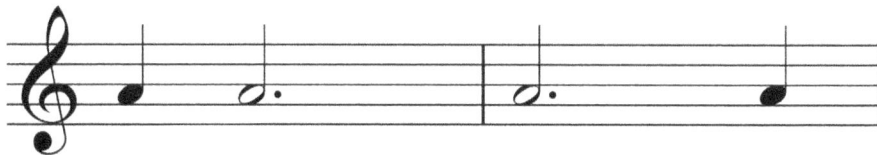

681

do   bou   duo   bo

683

duo   bo   duo   bo

685

bu   bo   duo   bo

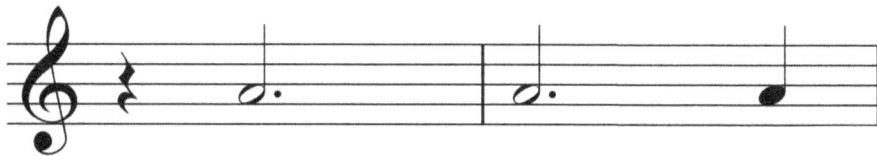

687

so   bou   duo   bo

689

do   bu   bo   so   bu   bo

691

do   bou   so   bu   bo

693

duo   bo   so   bu   bo

695

so   bu   bo   so   bu   bo

697

so   bou   so   bu   bo

699

do   bu   bo   so   bou

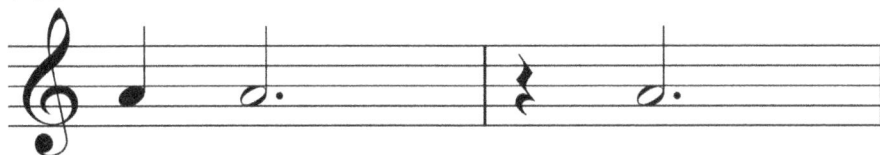

701

do   bou   so   bou

703

duo   bo   so   bou

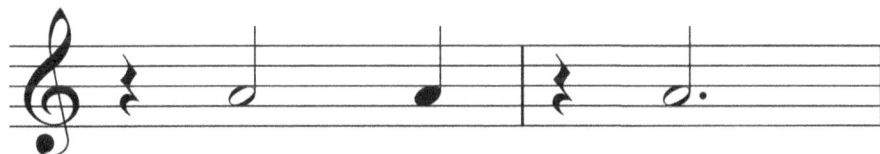

705

so   bu   bo   so   bou

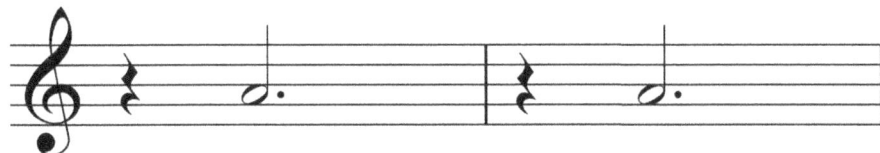

707

so   bou   so   bou

709

GG

do   bu   bo   do   bu   bo

711

do   bu   bo   do   bou

713

do   bu   bo   duo   bo

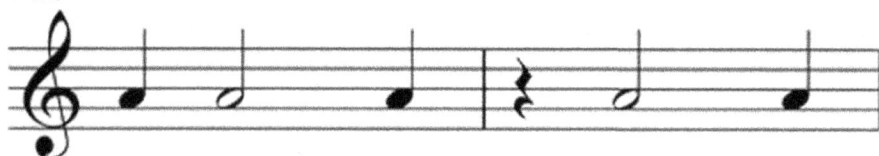

715

do   bu   bo   so   bu   bo

717

do   bu   bo   so   bou

719

do   bou   do   bu   bo

721

do   bou   do   bou

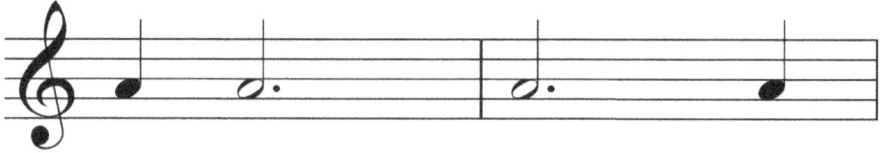

723

do   bou   duo   bo

725

do   bou   so   bu   bo

727

do   bou   so   bou

729

duo   bo   do   bu   bo

731

duo   bo   do   bou

733

duo   bo   duo   bo

735

duo   bo   so   bu   bo

737

duo   bo   so   bou

739

so bu bo do bu bo

741

so bu bo do bou

743

so bu bo duo bo

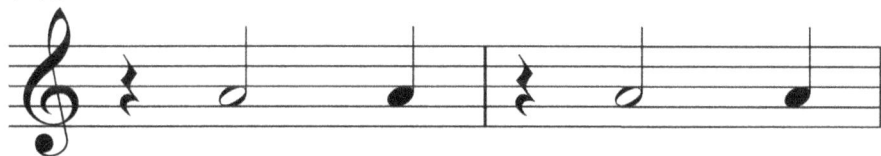

745

so bu bo so bu bo

747

so bu bo so bou

749

so   bou   do   bu   bo

751

so   bou   do   bou

753

so   bou   duo   bo

755

so   bou   so   bu   bo

757

so   bou   so   bou

Chapter Ten: What You Have Learned

Congratulations! You have learned a lot through learning and talking dobodobo.

You learned a one bar dobodobo rhythm.

You learned a vocabulary of sixteen dobodobo quarter note rhythms, one word at time. You learned that fifteen of these rhythms *derived* from the one bar dobodobo rhythm.

You learned to talk the dobodobo vocabulary through 373 two bar phrases.

You talked each dobodobo rhythm several times in different contexts.

You talked dobodobo 32 times across the 758 bars.

You talked 3 attack, dobodobo rhythms, one hundred and eighty-five times: namely, dobobu 41 times, dobubo 62 times, dudobo 41 times and sobodobo, 41 times.

You talked 2 attack, dobodobo rhythms, three hundred and twenty-one times: specifically, dobou 65 times, dubu 44 times, duobo 64 times, sobobu 38 times, sobubo 66 times and sudobo, 44 times.

You talked 1 attack, dobodobo rhythms, one hundred and eighty-five times: specifically, de 21 times, be 20 times, sobou 62 times, subu 41 times and suobo, 41 times. Finally you talked se 35 times.

The net result of all this activity is that you have had a thorough dobodobo experience. You spent 758 bars talking a sixteen bar dobodobo vocabulary in 373 different combinations.

You talked nine chapters of dobodobo rhythms, one **rhythm density** at a time. Within each chapter you talked different **rhythm profiles** and explored all the possibilities within one rhythm density level.

You talked one 8 attack rhythm, eight 7 attack rhythms, forty-four 6 attack rhythms, fifty-six 5 attack rhythms, one hundred 4 attack rhythms, fifty-eight 3 attack rhythms, forty-seven 2 attack rhythms, ten 1 attack rhythms and fifty-five syncopated rhythms.

You learned that each density level could be broken down to **attack profiles.** For example, 7 attack rhythms could be organised as 3 attack plus 4 attack rhythm profiles (3 + 4) and vice versa (4 + 3).

You learned how the principle of **rhythm alternation** (strong event alternating with weak event), along with the concept of **rhythm density,** can help you predict, and reflect on, the rhythm impact of any phrase.

In short, you have learned and talked the dobodobo's. You are now comfortable cutting and slicing dobodobo, in sixteen different ways, in 373 different contexts. That is no small achievement.

But there's more.

In talking these dobodobo rhythms, you have trained your **ear** to hear these rhythms as rhythmisation words. You have trained your **eye** to see these rhythms as rhythmisation words and notation. You have trained your **speech** to say them on demand in any dobodobo context. These are important achievements that you can—rightfully--celebrate.

The next stage is to embed these dobodobo rhythms as *physiological* instructions, in your body, *off* your instrument. The stage after that is to embed them as physiological instructions, in your body, *on* your instrument.

The objective of this book is to *install these dobodobo rhythms in your mind and speech* and to get you to talk all the rhythms once from bar 01 to 758. If you have done that, then that goal is achieved. Well done.

Now you can read this book again, and again, following along with the section, entitled How Long To Read This Book, on page XX in the appendices. Or, you can proceed directly to talking your way through Rhythm Book 102 Eighth Note Rhythm Patterns for All Musicians

Thank you for your interest and time. Thank you for reading this far. Thank you for making dobodobo part of your rhythm foundation.

How To Learn Dobodobo Words

Learn Sixteen Dobodobo Words in 8 Bar Sections

In this section you will introduce the sixteen word vocabulary to your mind, brain and speech system. You will teach yourself, step by step, to say and talk the following sixteen dobodobo words.

4 attack word: dobodobo.

3 attack words: dobobu, dobubo, dudobo, sobodobo.

2 attack words: dobou, dubu, duobo, sobobu, sobubo, sudobo.

1 attack words: de, sobou, subu, suobo.

0 attack word: se.

So let's get started.

Step 01: Set your metronome to MM60. Pronounce the vowel o as in go. Say dobodobo 8 times like this. Each syllable is held for one full click.

Dobodobo dobodobo dobodobo dobodobo
Dobodobo dobodobo dobodobo dobodobo

Then rest your mind for 8 clicks. Then take 8 clicks to prepare your mind and speech system to say the next rhythm in the next step.

Step 02: Say dubu 8 times as directed below. Pronounce the u vowel as in blue. Each syllable is held for two full clicks. Ensure you hold du and bu for the full two clicks.

Dubu dubu dubu dubu
Dubu dubu dubu dubu

Then rest your mind for 8 clicks. Then take 8 clicks to prepare your mind and speech system to say the next rhythm in the next step.

Step 03: Say de be 4 times as follows. Pronounce the e vowel as in bed. Each syllable is held for four full clicks. Ensure you hold de and be for the full 4 clicks. Breathe like a singer or wind instrument player.

De be de be
De be de be

Then rest your mind for 8 clicks. Then take 8 clicks to prepare your mind and speech system to say the next rhythm in the next step.

Step 04: Say dobobu 8 times as follows. Ensure you hold bu for the full two clicks.

Dobobu dobobu dobobu dobobu
Dobobu dobobu dobobu dobobu

Then rest your mind for 8 clicks. Then take 8 clicks to prepare your mind and speech system to say the next rhythm in the next step.

Step 05: Say dobubo 8 times as follows. Ensure you hold bu for the full two clicks.

Dobubo dobubo dobubo dobubo
Dobubo dobubo dobubo dobubo

Then rest your mind for 8 clicks. Then take 8 clicks to prepare your mind and speech system to say the next rhythm in the next step.

Step 06: Say dudobo 8 times as follows. Ensure you hold du for the full two clicks.

Dudobo dudobo dudobo dudobo
Dudobo dudobo dudobo dudobo

Then rest your mind for 8 clicks. Then take 8 clicks to prepare your mind and speech system to say the next rhythm in the next step.

Step 07: Say sobodobo 8 times as follows.

Sobodobo sobodobo sobodobo sobodobo
Sobodobo sobodobo sobodobo sobodobo

Then rest your mind for 8 clicks. Then take 8 clicks to prepare your mind and speech system to say the next rhythm in the next step.

Step 08: Say dobou 8 times as follows. Ensure you hold bou for the full three clicks.

Dobou dobou dobou dobou
Dobou dobou dobou dobou

Then rest your mind for 8 clicks. Then take 8 clicks to prepare your mind and speech system to say the next rhythm in the next step.

Step 09: Say duobo 8 times as follows. Ensure you hold duo for the full three clicks.

Duobo duobo duobo duobo
Duobo duobo duobo duobo

Then rest your mind for 8 clicks. Then take 8 clicks to prepare your mind and speech system to say the next rhythm in the next step.

Step 10: Say sobobu 8 times as follows. Ensure you hold bu for the full two clicks.

Sobobu sobobu sobobu sobobu
Sobobu sobobu sobobu sobobu

Then rest your mind for 8 clicks. Then take 8 clicks to prepare your mind and speech system to say the next rhythm in the next step.

Step 11: Say sobubo 8 times as follows. Ensure you hold bu for the full 2 clicks.

Sobubo sobubo sobubo sobubo
Sobubo sobubo sobubo sobubo

Then rest your mind for 8 clicks. Then take 8 clicks to prepare your mind and speech system to say the next rhythm in the next step.

Step 12: Say sudobo 8 times as follows. Ensure you hold su for the full two clicks.

Sudobo sudobo sudobo sudobo
Sudobo sudobo sudobo sudobo

Then rest your mind for 8 clicks. Then take 8 clicks to prepare your mind and speech system to say the next rhythm in the next step.

Step 13: Say sobou 8 times as follows. Ensure you hold bou for the full three clicks.

Sobou sobou sobou sobou
Sobou sobou sobou sobou

Then rest your mind for 8 clicks. Then take 8 clicks to prepare your mind and speech system to say the next rhythm in the next step.

Step 14: Say subu 8 times as follows. Ensure you hold su and bu for the full two clicks.

Subu subu subu subu
Subu subu subu subu

Then rest your mind for 8 clicks. Then take 8 clicks to prepare your mind and speech system to say the next rhythm in the next step.

Step 15: Say suobo 8 times as follows. Ensure you hold suo for the full three clicks.

Suobo suobo suobo suobo
Suobo suobo suobo suobo

Then rest your mind for 8 clicks. Then take 8 clicks to prepare your mind and speech system to say the next rhythm in the next step.

Step 16: Say se 8 times as follows. Ensure you hold se for the full four clicks.

Se se se se
Se se se se

Turn off the metronome. Relax.

Step 17: Take a 2 minute rest. Let your mind wander. Let your subconscious librarians archive all the learning you have just done for convenient retrieval in the future. Let your mind save everything to disc. Acknowledge your mind has just done concentrated work and that it has earned a, well deserved, rest.

Learn Sixteen Dobodobo Sounds with Notation Instructions

In the following nine pages, you can simply set your metronome to MM60 and read and talk along with the notation and rhythmisation.

Learn Dobodobo Sounds

♩ = 60

do bo do bo   do bo do bo   do bo do bo   do bo do bo

5

do bo do bo   do bo do bo   do bo do bo   do bo do bo

9

Rest for 8 clicks   Mentally prepare next rhythm for 8 clicks

13

du   bu   du   bu   du   bu   du   bu

17

du   bu   du   bu   du   bu   du   bu

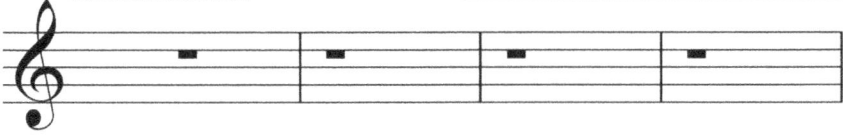

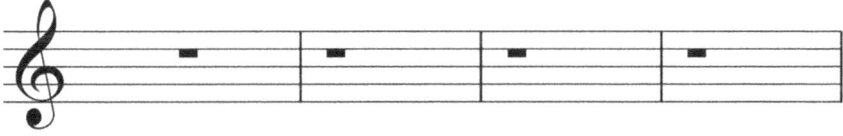

41

do bo bu   do bo bu   do bo bu   do bo bu

45 | Rest for 8 clicks | Mentally prepare next rhythm for 8 clicks

49

do bu bo   do bu bo   do bu bo   do bu bo

53

do bu bo   do bu bo   do bu bo   do bu bo

57 | Rest for 8 clicks | Mentally prepare next rhythm for 8 clicks

VIII

61

du   do bo   du   do bo   du   do bo   du   do bo

65

du   do bo   du   do bo   du   do bo   du   do bo

69

Rest for 8 clicks   Mentally prepare next rhythm for 8 clicks

73

so bo do bo   so bo do bo   so bo do bo   so bo do bo

77

so bo do bo   so bo do bo   so bo do bo   so bo do bo

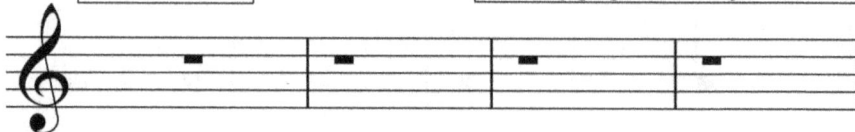

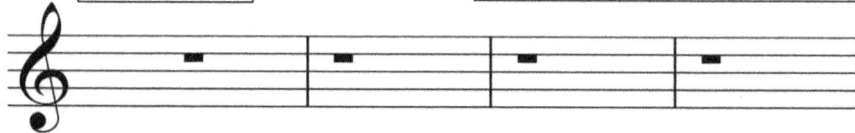

101

duo   bo   duo   bo   duo   bo   duo   bo

105   Rest for 8 clicks   Mentally prepare next rhythm for 8 clicks

109

so bo bu   so bo bu   so bo bu   so bo bu

113

so bo bu   so bo bu   so bo bu   so bo bu

117   Rest for 8 clicks   Mentally prepare next rhythm for 8 clicks

121

so bu bo   so bu bo   so bu bo   so bu bo

125

so bu bo   so bu bo   so bu bo   so bu bo

129 Rest for 8 clicks   Mentally prepare next rhythm for 8 clicks

133

su do bo   su do bo   su do bo   su do bo

137

su do bo   su do bo   su do bo   su do bo

141 Rest for 8 clicks   Mentally prepare next rhythm for 8 clicks

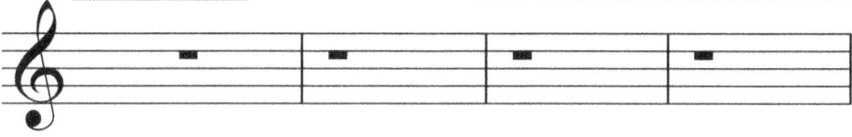

145

so   bou   so   bou   so   bou   so   bou

149

so   bou   so   bou   so   bou   so   bou

153 Rest for 8 clicks   Mentally prepare next rhythm for 8 clicks

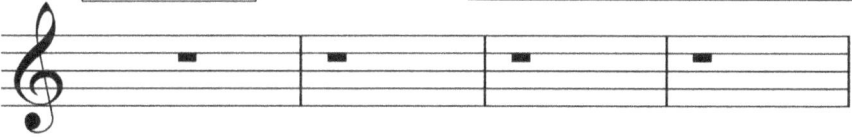

157

su   bu   su   bu   su   bu   su   bu

161

su   bu   su   bu   su   bu   su   bu

165   Rest for 8 clicks   Mentally prepare next rhythm for 8 clicks

169

suo   bo   suo   bo   suo   bo   suo   bo

173

suo   bo   suo   bo   suo   bo   suo   bo

177   Rest for 16 clicks

Now that you have learned this vocabulary, you can start talking and reading the rhythm phrases section.

Or, if you need more work learning the dobodobo words before proceeding, you can do one, or all, of the following three processes.

Learn Sixteen Dobodobo Words in 12 Bar Sections

Repeat the previous exercise with 12 repetitions instead of 8. The objectives are twofold. One, is to give you practice at isolating and saying each rhythm. Two, to give you experience saying the rhythm within the 12 bar blues form.

You will feel a 12 bar form as you say the rhythm 12 times. You will feel the form as well as the surface rhythm. Being able to feel a form makes getting lost---when you are jamming or improvising--*so* much harder.

Learn Sixteen Dobodobo Words in 16 Bar Sections

Repeat the previous exercise with 16 repetitions instead of 12. The objectives are the same. One objective is to give you practise at isolating and saying each rhythm. The second objective is to give you experience saying the rhythm within a 16 bar form.

Sixteen bars is typically the length of two verses or a bridge and last verse in typical standard jazz and pop tunes. Again you are feeling form as well as surface rhythm. Very cool.

Learn Sixteen Dobodobo Words in 32 Bar Sections

Repeat the previous exercise with 32 repetitions instead of 16. The twofold objectives remain the same. The first aim is to give you practise at isolating and saying each rhythm. The second goal is to give you experience saying the rhythm within a thirty-two bar form.

Thirty-two bars is the typical length of a standard jazz and pop tune. Be aware that you are feeling form as well as surface rhythm when you repeat any dobodobo rhythm 32 times.

Frequently Asked Questions

Why does saying the d and b in the prescribed place matter?

Whenever you say do, du, duo or de you are saying an event that starts on the strong beat, the strong half of the bar or on the strong bar. Whenever you say bo, bu, bou or be you are saying an event that starts on the weak beat, the weak half of the bar or on the weak bar.

By specifying whether any rhythm is a weak or strong event (the same rhythm can be weak or strong) you are mindful of the principle of rhythmic alternation operating. Knowing whether events are weak or strong enables you to feel surface and underlying rhythm *simultaneously.*

In short, the specific consonants are signposts that prevent you from getting lost in any music you are playing. And when you do get lost, they help you quickly find your place again.

How does saying the d and b in the prescribed place help a rhythm guitar player?

Any d led syllable means you down pick or down strum that syllable. Any b led syllable means you up pick or up strum that syllable. In other words, the consonants are specific picking and strumming instructions.

How is each rhythm derived from dobodobo?

Each surface dobodobo rhythm is related to the underlying rhythm by between one to six steps.

I'll simply list each rhythm and their derivations from dobodobo to surface rhythm.

I'll walk you through the steps for two of the sixteen rhythms.

Example 01: dobodobo > dobo_obo > doboobo > dobubo

For the **dobubo** rhythm, start with dobodobo, remove the third consonant to read dobo_obo, combine o_o into oo then combine oo into a u vowel to now read dobubo.

Example 02: dobodobo > do_odo_o > doodoo > dudu > dubu

For the **dubu** rhythm, start with dobodobo, remove the second and fourth consonants to now read do_odo_o, rewrite o_o as oo then rewrite oo as a u vowel to now read dudu, then comply with the principle of alternation and rewrite as du bu

Here are the remaining dobodobo rhythms with their derivations from dobodobo.

3 attack rhythms

dobodobo > dobodo_o > dobodoo > dobodu > dobobu >

dobodobo> dobo_obo > doboobo > dobubo

dobodobo > do_odobo > doodobo > dudobo

dobodobo > sobodobo

2 attack rhythms

dobodobo > dobo_o_o > dobo_oo > dobo_u > dobou

dobodobo > do_odo_o > doodoo > dudu > dubu

dobodobo > do_o_obo > doo_obo > du_obo > duobo

dobodobo > dobodo_o > dobodoo > dobodu > dobobu > sobobu

dobodobo > dobo_obo > doboobo > dobubo > sobubo

dobodobo > do_odobo > doodobo > dudobo > sudobo

1 attack rhythms

dobodobo > do_o_ o _o > doo_oo > du_u > duu > de

dobodobo > dobo_o_o > dobo_u > dobou > sobou

dobodobo > do_odo_o > doodoo > dudu > dubu > subu

dobodobo > do_o_obo > doo_obo > du_obo > duobo > suobo >

These derivations give you a detailed understanding of how each rhythm derives from dobodobo, how they all belong to the dobodobo vocabulary and in what specific sense they can each be called a dobodobo rhythm.

Do I keep the tempo in my hands or feet?

Keep the tempo in your feet. Keep the melodic rhythm in your speech and/or hands. In this book you are talking melodic rhythm.

What tempo rhythm should I use?

In the beginning, most rhythmisation students default to a dobodobo tempo rhythm so that their feet and speech are using the same rhythm level. If you want a stiff rhythm effect, this is a good solution.

If you want a flowing rhythm effect, then, play dubudubu in your feet while you talk dobodobo. This is the first tempo rhythm you should learn and practise. Firstly, play dubudubu rhythm tempo in your feet, with a metronome set to a dobodobo tempo, while you talk dobodobo. Secondly, repeat the same process without a metronome.

If you want an even more confident rhythm effect, then play debedebe in your feet while you talk dobodobo. Firstly, play debedebe rhythm tempo in your feet, with a metronome set to a dobodobo tempo, while you talk dobodobo. Secondly, repeat the same process without a metronome.

By training your feet to play dubudubu or debedebe while talking dobodobo, you are teaching yourself to master tempo rhythm and melodic rhythm *simultaneously*. The place for dobodobo is in the melodic rhythm or the metronome click but not in the feet.

How long to read the whole book?

At a continuous tempo of MM60 it would take you 51 minutes to read every single bar the first time.

This book contains 3,032 beats of notation and rhythmisation. Your first task is to read through the book once. Then, periodically read, talk and play all the 8 attacks to 0 attack rhythms, and the syncopations, one session at a time.

This table below outlines how long (to the nearest minute) each session will take you at any given tempo. Take your time. Enjoy.

Example:
At a continuous tempo of MM84 it would take you 36 minutes to read every single bar.

Tempo	Minutes
MM 60	51
MM 64	47
MM 68	45
MM 72	42
MM 76	40
MM 80	38
MM 84	36
MM 88	34
MM 92	33
MM 96	32
MM 100	30
MM 104	29
MM 108	28
MM 112	27
MM 116	26
MM 120	25
MM 124	24

Do you count rhythm with rhythmisation?

Counting rhythm is one rhythm learning and measuring system and rhythmisation is another. You can use both systems. The author uses rhythm counting for *out* of tempo analysis and measurement of *static rhythm* and he uses rhythmisation for *in* tempo *dynamic* rhythm description. Rhythm counting describes only the attack and not the duration of any rhythm whereas rhythmisation describes both. Saying any rhythm word with the correct vowel duration *automatically* gives you the correct rhythm. The author uses rhythmisation over ninety-five percent of the time and uses counting, the other five percent of the time, to help new students to get started with rhythmisation.

Is Rhythmisation the only rhythm verbalisation system?

No. There are several others: some new, some centuries old. The Carnatic vocal system of Konnokol or Solkattu is an old rhythm verbalisation system. In her 1998 Masters in Music Performance thesis entitled "KONNAKOL The History and Development of Solkattu - the Vocal Syllables - of the Mridangam", Lisa Young gives you a well documented introduction. For more information, visit www.lisayoung.com.au

Another verbalisation system gaining traction in the west is Takadimi. The Takadimi system of rhythm pedagogy is described in "Takadimi: A Beat-Oriented System of Rhythm Pedagogy," Journal of Music Theory Pedagogy, 1996, by Hoffman, Pelto, and White. For more information, visit www.takadimi.net.

Rhythmisation was first taught in Auckland, New Zealand, in 1982, some 14 years before the cited Konnokol and Takadimi works were published and 17 years before the author gained, dial up, internet access in 1999.

Some African rhythm verbalisation traditions are described in African Rhythm and African Sensibility, by John Miller Chernoff.

There are other rhythmisation systems used in primary and secondary schools including Kodaly, Orff and Edward E. Gordon, amongst others.

How does knowing dobodobo help the jazz, rock and pop musician?

The first thing you need to be able to do, in western commercial music, is keep the beat. Being able to keep the beat through any dobodobo rhythm is the most basic music skill required.

Rockers, jazzers and pop musicians deal mostly in dabadaba eighth note melodic rhythms. These rhythms are divisions of what? They are divisions of the dobodobo or quarter note rhythm. When you know your dobodobo's you can divide them into dabadaba's. When you don't know them you can't.

How does knowing dobodobo help the blues and reggae musician?

Blues and reggae styles are largely characterised by dibidibi melodic rhythms. Dibidibi rhythms are divisions of the dabadaba rhythms and subdivisions of the dobodobo rhythms. When you know your dobodobo's you can divide them into dabadaba eighth notes, and subdivide them into dibidibi sixteenth notes.

The most convincing dibidibi performances are those supported by a strong dabadaba framework which is, in turn, supported by a strong dobodobo framework.

The wimpiest sixteenth note rhythm performances are those that are not supported by strong dabadaba and dobodobo frameworks.

How does dobodobo help with odd subdivisions?

Dobodobo provides you with the framework you need to be able to subdivide any quarter note into any triplet, quintuplet and septuplet value.

What is the principle of rhythmic alternation?

Alternation in music reflects alternations that occur in the natural world: alternating tides coming in and out, sun rising and setting, moon rising and setting, up and down, happy and sad and so on.

The key rhythmic alternation in music is strong versus weak.

Strong bars (odd numbered bars) versus weak bars (even numbered bars). Strong beats (odd numbered beats) versus weak beats (even numbered beats). Strong beat divisions versus weak beat divisions. Strong beat subdivisions versus weak beat subdivisions.

Rhythmic alternations are also denoted by terms like, off and on the beat, the downbeat and the upbeat.

Understanding the principle of rhythmic alternation greatly benefits you in many ways, including expanding your rhythmic awareness, deepening your rhythmic sensitivity and better equipping you to write and play strong melody.

The hierarchy of strong-weak rhythm alternation is displayed here.

		S				W		
	S		S		S		S	
S	W	S	W	S	W	S	W	

For the purposes of dobodobo you can think of the three S W levels from top to bottom as representing de be, dividing into du bu du bu, dividing into do bo do bo do bo do bo — as displayed in the next table.

	de				be		
du		bu		du		bu	
do	bo	do	bo	do	bo	do	bo

What's an example of a dobodobo song?

Autumn Leaves by Johnny Mercer is an example of a dobodobo song. The melodic rhythm is rhythmised as one bar phrases.

P
sobodobo
A
de~obodobo dubu~obodobo
de~obodobo de~obodobo
B
de~obodobo dubu~obodobo
de~obodobo de~obodobo
C
dobobu~obodobo de~obodobo
de~obodobo de~osodobo
D
dobodobo duobo dubu~uobo
duobo dudobo de sobodobo

Key: P means pick up bar, A means verse 1, B means verse 2. C means chorus, D means verse 3.

Note: The tilde ~ symbol can occur between two vowels in the same duration. The presence of a barline, occurring between vowels in the same diphthong, is indicated by the tilde ~ symbol.

Rhythmisation Glossary

Term	Definition
1e+a	The name of a rhythm counting system.
Attack	Where the duration of a rhythm starts. In rhythmisation an attack is indicated by a consonant.
Attacks	The number of sounded consonants in a rhythm word.
Attack Profile	A synonym for rhythm profile
Call and Response	A rhythm phrase where one rhythm calls and another rhythm answers in response. The phrase could be of any length, usually four bars or less.
Click	A metronome click.
Calling Rhythm	The first rhythm in a call and response rhythm phrase. The calling rhythm occurs on the strong part of the phrase.
Counting Rhythm	A system for identifying rhythm attack patterns but not durations.
Dababa Dababa	The name of the triple eighth note rhythmisation vocabulary in 6/8.
Dabadaba	The name of the eighth note rhythmisation vocabulary in 2/4.
Dabadaba	The eighth note rhythm level.
Dabadaba Dabadaba	The name of the eighth note rhythmisation vocabulary in 4/4.
Dabadabadaba	The name of the eighth note rhythmisation vocabulary in 3/4.
Debedebe	The name of the whole note rhythmisation vocabulary in 4/4.
Debedebe	The whole note rhythm level.

Dibidibi	The name of the sixteenth note rhythmisation vocabulary in 1/4.
Dibidibi	The sixteenth note rhythm level.
DibibiDibibi	The name of the triple sixteenth note rhythmisation vocabulary in 1/4.
Dibidibi Dibidibi	The name of the sixteenth note rhythmisation vocabulary in 2/4.
Diphthong	A co-occurrence of two or more vowels.
Diphthong Rhythm	A duration containing two or more different vowels indicating equivalence to dotted or tied notation rhythms or syncopated rhythms.
Dobobo	The name of the triplet quarter note rhythmisation vocabulary in 3/4.
Dobodobo	The name of the quarter note rhythmisation vocabulary in 4/4.
Dobodobo	The quarter note rhythm level.
Dububu	The name of the triplet half note rhythmisation vocabulary in 3/2.
Dubudubu	The name of the half note rhythmisation vocabulary in 4/4.
Dubudubu	The half note rhythm level.
Dynamic Rhythm	Rhythm in tempo.
Harmonic Rhythm	The rhythm level or vocabulary used by the harmony or chord changes in a song. Debe, dubu and duobo are the most common harmonic rhythms.
Main Rhythm	Refers to the most frequent rhythm vocabulary used in a piece of music.
Melodic Rhythm	The rhythm (level or vocabulary) used by the melody.
Parent rhythm	A synonym for seed rhythm.

Pataka	The triplet eighth note rhythm level.
Pataka Pataka	The name of the triplet eighth note rhythmisation vocabulary in 2/4.
Pataka Pataka Pataka Pataka	The name of the triplet eighth note rhythmisation vocabulary in 4/4.
Pitiki	The triplet sixteenth note rhythm level.
Pitiki Pitiki	The name of the triplet sixteenth note rhythmisation vocabulary in 1/4
Pitiki Pitiki Pitiki Pitiki	The name of the triplet sixteenth note rhythmisation vocabulary in 2/4.
Potoko	The triplet quarter note rhythm level.
Potoko Potoko	The triplet quarter note rhythm vocabulary.
Putuku	The triplet half note rhythm level.
Putuku Putuku	The triplet half note rhythm vocabulary.
Response Rhythm	The rhythm that answers a calling rhythm in a call and response phrase.
Rhythm Balance	Refers to the balance between phrases within a rhythm profile. For example which balance do you want for a 7A, 2 bar rhythm phrase? 7+0, 6+1, 5+2, 4+3, 3+4, 2+5, 1+6 or 0+7? Which bar do you want to have the most rhythm attacks in? The strong or weak bar?
Rhythm Density	Refers to the number of attacks—or sounded consonants--in a rhythm or rhythm phrase. A 7A attack rhythm means there are 7 attacks (7 sounded consonants) in the phrase. Rhythm Density gives you an idea of how active a given rhythm phrase is.

Rhythm Profile	A more detailed description of rhythm density. For example, 2 bar, 7 attack rhythms can be broken into the following rhythm profiles: 7+0, 6+1, 5+2, 4+3, 3+4, 2+5, 1+6, 0+7.
Rhythm Level	Refers to the *level* of the whole note, half note, quarter note, eighth note or sixteenth note or triplet whole note, triplet half note, triplet quarter note, triplet eighth note or triplet sixteenth note. Any one of these values is a rhythm level.
Rhythm Phrase	A sequence of rhythm words.
Rhythm Position	The position of any rhythm event in the bar or phrase. Rhythm counting counts four quarter notes as 1 2 3 4. Each numeral denotes the ordinal position of each quarter note. Dobodobo describes the same rhythm. The consonants d and b, respectively, denote the strong and weak position of each quarter note in the phrase. You can use both approaches interchangeably.
Rhythm Resolution	A smallest rhythm level used in a composition. For example, a song may be mostly dobodobo but there are three dibidibi bars included. The rhythm resolution for this song is dibidibi.
Rhythm Substitution	Any act of substituting one rhythm for another. You may substitute any rhythm with a rhythm from the same or different profile in the same or different rhythm density, according to the degree of similarity or difference you want to achieve.
Rhythm Variation	Similar to rhythm substitution.

Rhythm Vocabulary	Any group of rhythms derived from a seed rhythm or a parent rhythm. Any rhythm can be both a seed rhythm for one vocabulary and a derived rhythm in other vocabularies.
Rhythm Weighting	Synonym for rhythm balance.
Rhythm Word	A sequence of rhythmisation syllables.
Rhythmic Alternation	The underlying rhythm alternation between strong and weak events on any rhythm level.
Rhythmisation	Rhythmisation is the term coined by Taura Eruera to denote a system for verbalising rhythm with syllables (rather than numbers) and writing rhythm in simple English text, rather than music notation.
Rhythmisation Consonant b	The b consonant precedes any sounded vowel or diphthong that occurs on a weak duple rhythm position, division or subdivision.
Rhythmisation Consonant d	The d consonant precedes any sounded vowel or diphthong that occurs on a strong duple rhythm position, division or subdivision.
Rhythmisation Consonant k	The k consonant precedes any sounded vowel or diphthong that occurs on the third triplet rhythm position, division or subdivision.
Rhythmisation Consonant p	The p consonant precedes any sounded vowel or diphthong that occurs on the first triplet rhythm position, division or subdivision.

Rhythmisation Consonant s	The s consonant precedes any silent or unsounded vowel or diphthong that occurs on any duple rhythm position, division or subdivision, strong or weak.
Rhythmisation Consonant t	The t consonant precedes any sounded vowel or diphthong that occurs on the second triplet rhythm position, division or subdivision.
Rhythmisation Consonant z	The z consonant precedes any silent or unsounded vowel or diphthong that occurs on any triplet position, division or subdivision, strong or weak.
Rhythmisation Consonants	The main rhythmisation consonants are d, b, s, p, t, k, z.
Rhythmisation Text	When rhythm is written out in plain English text rather than notation.
Rhythmisation Vowel a	a (as in path) to indicate eighth note duration.
Rhythmisation Vowel e	e (as in bed) to indicate whole note duration.
Rhythmisation Vowel i	i (as in beat) to indicate sixteenth note duration.
Rhythmisation Vowel o	o (as in go) to indicate quarter note duration.
Rhythmisation Vowel u	u (as in blue) to indicate half note duration.
Rhythmisation Vowels	The five main rhythmisation vowels are: a, e, i, o, u.
Rhythmisations	A sequence of rhythmisation syllables, words and phrases
Rhythmise	The process of rhythmising rhythm notation into rhythmisation

Rhythmiser	Somebody who rhythmises.
Rhythmising	The process of verbalising rhythm with rhythmisation consonants and vowels.
Secondary Rhythm	The second most frequent rhythm in a piece, which generally, occupies less than 20% of the piece.
Seed Rhythm	Any single rhythm that a vocabulary is derived from.
Solmisation	Solmisation represents pitch with syllables rather than notation. India has used solmisation systems since 1300-1000 BC while Guido D'Arezzo created the solmisation do-re-mi system in the 10th century.
Static Rhythm	Rhythm that is written down or analysed out of tempo.
Syncopation	Indicated by diphthongs or co-occurring different vowels in the same duration..
Syncopation Density	The number of consecutive syncopated events in a phrase. For example, there is a 5S sequence in a 9A rhythm. That is, there are 5 syncopated events in a 9 attack rhythm.
Tempo Rhythm	The rhythm level that is kept in the foot and is usually twice as long as the melodic rhythm level.
Tertiary rhythm	The third most used rhythm vocabulary in a piece, which generally, occupies less than 5% of the piece.
Tilde	This symbol ~ occurs between two vowels in a diphthong to indicate where a bar line occurs in a duration.

About the Author

I am Taura Eruera and I live in Grey Lynn, Auckland, New Zealand. Apart from a decade off in the 90's I have taught guitar continuously since 1982. That experience included teaching harmony, rhythm and guitar at the School of Creative Musicianship for six years followed by private teaching, seminars and clinics.

Over the years I have written many titles for guitar, melody, harmony and rhythm instruction. My titles have been self-published for in-house and private student consumption or for publication on self-owned websites. Over this time my energy has been focused more on creation than distribution. Now with platforms like Amazon Kindle available, I am formatting my catalogue of work for wider distribution.

Much of my writing has come out of my studies with Dick Grove, Howard Roberts and, more importantly, directly out of my teaching experience. I am grateful to a crazy diamond of a guitar player named Clash for being my pioneer rhythmisation dabadaba student, way back in the day. Clash reckoned that his skill in verbalising the Dabadaba's enabled him to put his strumming and picking hand on auto pilot, which made life that much easier for him at the Guitar Institute of Technology.

Guitar teaching has been a major activity for me over the years. Teaching has always alternated with gigging and other activities in my work life: old school, session work before the computer; transcription and lead sheet preparation and digital session work after computers came in.

Activities outside guitar teaching extended to business consultation, business startups, founding roles in radio and health care companies, software development and search engine optimization services.

Even though I am involved in many interests, guitar teaching remains an important part of my week. Writing up those insights remains an important part of my teaching.

Join Rhythmisation Insights

Thank you for reading this book. I hope you find this book useful and thorough. Let me invite you to join the Rhythmisation Insights Group.

Simply paste this URL into your web browser -- https://tinyurl.com/dobodobo101

You will be redirected to a page where you can enter your details in the sign up form and join the discoveries!

Expect lots of useful information that we just couldn't include in this book. Expect real life resources from real people, like you, sharing their experiences and insights with you. Expect a lot of your questions to be discussed, shared and answered. See you on the inside.

Kind regards,
Taura

www.ingramcontent.com/pod-product-compliance
Lightning Source LLC
Chambersburg PA
CBHW021128020426
42331CB00005B/664